Communication and the World of Work

Christopher Beddows MSc (Ed)

Senior Lecturer
English and Communications Studies
Nelson and Colne College

McGRAW-HILL BOOK COMPANY

London · New York · St Louis · San Francisco · Auckland · Bogotá · Guatemala
Hamburg · Lisbon · Madrid · Mexico · Montreal · New Delhi · Panama · Paris
San Juan · São Paulo · Singapore · Sydney · Tokyo · Toronto

Published by
McGRAW-HILL Book Company (UK) Limited
MAIDENHEAD · BERKSHIRE · ENGLAND

British Library Cataloguing in Publication Data

Beddows, Christopher
  Communication and the world of work.
  1. Communication – For business studies
  I. Title
  001.51′024658

ISBN 0-07-707107-7

123 WL 898

Typeset by Gecko Limited, Bicester
and printed and bound in Great Britain by Thomson Litho Ltd, East Kilbride,
Scotland

Contents

Introduction

This book does not pretend to be the definitive text that is guaranteed to lead to inevitable success in business examinations. I make no apology, however, as no such book can exist. Although the material can be used by a student studying without the support of a teacher and classroom colleagues, it is best used to complement the work done on a course by an experienced teacher.

The material is organized as a series of alternating chapters dealing with communication theory in business followed by 'twin' case studies. The case studies allow the student reader to follow two assistants, new to the world of business, who are working in a manufacturing and a service company respectively. They are seen trying to put the theory they have recently learned into practice.

Activity and assignment exercises of a practical and syllabus-orientated type are found throughout the text as well as sections on grammar and language use. These last sections go over essential ground that should have been covered at the GCSE stage but about which experience suggests students need reminding.

Teachers will find that the ground is covered extensively rather than intensively and there are many points which can be expanded upon to the students' benefit and which will allow teachers to exploit their particular expertise.

The material has been put together as a result of a widespread demand voiced by teachers of BTEC, CPVE and RSA courses for alternative work to that currently available.

Christopher Beddows

For my students and my colleagues, but most of all for my family

1 Letters of application

A letter of application is possibly the most important letter you will ever write. Upon its success will depend your personal and financial future. Security, contentment and vocational achievement all stem from a careful, concise and accomplished letter of application. If the letter does not lead to an applicant being shortlisted, then all the personality and qualifications that may be possessed will remain hidden.

Assuming that the post applied for is suited to your age, experience and qualifications, then the following points should be remembered when writing a letter of application:

1. Unless you are specifically requested to write by hand or your writing is legible then the letter should be typed. It is probably better to type a letter applying for a post in a service or manufacturing company as your typing itself is part of the application.
2. The letter of application is a business letter and should be presented in the appropriate layout.
3. Spelling, punctuation and paragraphing should be checked with painstaking care.
4. The letter should be short enough to avoid boring the reader but long enough to impress with your fluency of language and suitability as an applicant.
5. The letter should not contain every single detail of your background or nothing will be left to discuss at interview.
6. The tone of the letter should be one of serious enthusiasm. Avoid excessive humility or colloquial brashness. The aim is to impress upon the reader that the applicant is sensible, enthusiastic and well qualified to take up the post offered.

Here is an advertisement for a post with a small, local travel agency.

REQUIRED IMMEDIATELY –

COUNTER CLERK

FOR WORK WITH WELL-ESTABLISHED LOCAL TRAVEL AGENCY. APPLICANT SHOULD BE QUALIFIED UP TO GCSE/RSA 2 LEVEL AND HAVE PLEASANT PERSONALITY. SOME EXPERIENCE IN DEALING WITH THE PUBLIC AS WELL AS A BASIC KNOWLEDGE OF WORD PROCESSORS IS DESIRABLE.
REASONABLE SALARY FOR SUITABLE APPLICANT. LETTER OF APPLICATION TOGETHER WITH NAME AND ADDRESSES OF TWO REFEREES TO: MR ADAM BROWN, MANAGER, SPEEDY TRAVEL, MARKET STREET, LITTLEBOROUGH, WORCS. LB17 2PL.

Here are two letters that were received by Mr Brown in response to the advert.

Example 1

Roger Parkinson
17 Peter Street
Littleborough
Worcs

Dear Adam Brown

I saw your advert in the local paper recently which was about the job in your business. I'm your man! I stayed on at school till I was 16 and did a few GCSEs in the fifth form.

I've been working on my dad's market stall for a few months to earn enough money to get my motorbike back on the road. I could certainly do with some more cash than my dad gives me. I get on OK with most folks. What do you pay by the way?

My dad says he'll give me a reference and I should think that the careers fellow Mr Ratcliffe at the High School will do me one as well.

I can pop round any time at your convenience since I don't live that far from Peter Street.

Yours sincerly,

Roger Parkinson

P.S. I did geography at school up to the fourth form but then had to drop it 'cos of the options system. I know my way around anyway!

Comment 1

It goes almost without saying that this letter is totally inappropriate. Even if your have little or no experience of writing letters of application you will have noticed some of the more glaring faults. Here is a random list of the major errors:

1 The letter is not laid out in the form of a proper business letter (see following letter as an example).
2 The letter is undated.
3 The tone is cheeky and informal.
4 Few details are presented. We do not even know the age or qualifications of the applicant.
5 The referees' names and addresses are not presented clearly (and one's parent is never accepted as a referee!)
6 The paragraphs are haphazard and not thought out.
7 There has been no attempt to check the technical accuracy of the letter and the applicant does not know how to spell certain

key words or how to use apostrophes correctly.

8 The use of a PS (postscript) shows a lack of care in planning the letter and does not contain any useful information anyway.

This applicant would not get an interview. It is possible that he would do the job quite well but this letter ruins his chances.

Example 2

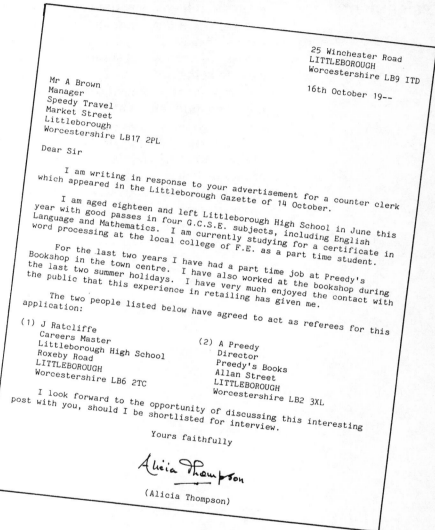

25 Winchester Road
LITTLEBOROUGH
Worcestershire LB9 ITD

16th October 19--

Mr A Brown
Manager
Speedy Travel
Market Street
Littleborough
Worcestershire LB17 2PL

Dear Sir

I am writing in response to your advertisement for a counter clerk which appeared in the Littleborough Gazette of 14 October.

I am aged eighteen and left Littleborough High School in June this year with good passes in four G.C.S.E. subjects, including English Language and Mathematics. I am currently studying for a certificate in word processing at the local college of F.E. as a part time student.

For the last two years I have had a part time job at Preedy's Bookshop in the town centre. I have also worked at the bookshop during the last two summer holidays. I have very much enjoyed the contact with the public that this experience in retailing has given me.

The two people listed below have agreed to act as referees for this application:

(1) J Ratcliffe
Careers Master
Littleborough High School
Roxeby Road
LITTLEBOROUGH
Worcestershire LB6 2TC

(2) A Preedy
Director
Preedy's Books
Allan Street
LITTLEBOROUGH
Worcestershire LB2 3XL

I look forward to the opportunity of discussing this interesting post with you, should I be shortlisted for interview.

Yours faithfully

Alicia Thompson

(Alicia Thompson)

Comment 2

This letter is much more likely to receive a favourable response. Its content and layout are concise and relevant to the post for which Alicia Thompson is applying.

1 The format is that of a standard business letter, with addresses placed appropriately.
2 The letter has been checked for spelling and punctuation errors.
3 The salutation ('Dear Sir') and complimentary close ('Yours faithfully') match and are punctuated correctly.
4 The names and addresses of the two referees are placed clearly as items in the letter. (They could have been placed separately after the signature as an addendum.)

5   The paragraphs are clear and contain separate but linked
     points of information.
6   The letter responds to all points mentioned in the original
     advertisement and approaches the desired tone of 'serious
     enthusiasm'.

Assignment

Even though you may not yet be planning an application for a job
it is a very good preliminary exercise to write some practice
letters. Have a look at the classified columns of your local
newspaper and select some job advertisements for which you are
close to being qualified. Underline those parts of the
advertisement that need responding to in your application. These
might include references to such matters as: experience,
qualifications, desired personality and subsidiary skills.

Write letters of application in a business format to two or three
of these advertisements. Mistakes that you make now and which
are correctible are not so important. What is important is that you
do not make similar mistakes when it comes to writing a 'real'
letter of application for a job.

2 Ongoing case studies

Sandra Kong

Sandra Kong served yet another portion of sweet and sour pork, curry sauce and chips, wrapped them up and forced a smile on to her face as she gave the customer his change. Business might be booming in her family's fast food takeaway, but her own efforts at getting a career in the business world were not reaping many rewards.

She thought back to the hard grind at the high school and the disappointing results in her GCSE exams. She remembered the move to the local college of FE and the CPVE course she had started. She smiled as she recalled the day her tutor had recommended her to transfer to a BTEC Business Studies course. At last she was on her way to a rewarding career – or so she thought.

Her results had been good, but, despite her qualifications, Sandra was still without a job. The problem was depressing. Only one interview had been forthcoming from nine applications so far.

Later that night she took stock of the situation. There was nothing wrong with her parents' business, but it wasn't what she wanted for herself. There had been too much training to throw it away working unsocial hours with no prospects of ever having to use her hard-won skills. But why wasn't she getting interviews? One out of nine didn't seem a very good rate.

Over a cup of coffee she carefully checked through the 'Situations Vacant' columns of the local newspaper. Her eye was drawn to an attractive boxed advert in a lower corner of the page.

It sounded interesting. It sounded more than interesting. It sounded ideal. She knew the company. It was just outside of town and had started off less than three years ago as a very small business that was run from the kitchen of a rather beautiful, old farmhouse. Their products were high-quality biscuits and cakes that had sold well locally. The owner had recognized the potential of his product and recently a modern factory extension had been built on to the farm and the delivery vans were seen far and wide. Sandra had even seen their attractively packaged biscuits for sale in some London shops when she had been to the capital on a college visit.

She read the advert again. It would be a good company to work for, but the more she read the advert the more frightening it seemed. Working for the managing director sounded full of prestige, but very demanding. She had a distinct crisis of confidence. Then Sandra remembered how frightened she had been when transferring from the CPVE course to the BTEC course. The nervousness had soon disappeared once she got

Rapidly expanding manufacturer of popular range of whole-food biscuits and confectionery requires

PERSONAL ASSISTANT

to work in close liaison with managing director.

The ideal applicant will be qualified up to BTEC standard and willing to adapt to the varying demands of a vigorous and active local manufacturing company.

Some experience of dealing with the general public would be desirable as well as willingness to learn new skills in a work situation. Reasonable salary and company pension scheme available to successful applicant. Apply in writing (with names and addresses of two referees) to:

A Botham
Personnel Officer
Honeypot Biscuits
Haworth Lane
Milham
Lancashire BB12 9PN

involved in the work and the same could happen again – if only she could get the job. She would have to get an interview first!

Sandra carefully cut out the Honeypot Biscuits advert from the paper and retired to her bedroom. It all depended on the letter. Rooting through her bookshelves she found the notes she had taken on her college course concerning letters of application. It all came back to her as she read the notes through carefully.

Since this was to be a most important letter, she jotted down on a note pad the main points she must ensure were contained in her letter. With the advert in front of her she jotted down her personal details that were relevant to the post offered.

1   Successful pass with good grades at BTEC level.
2   Details of part time and holiday jobs where meeting the general public was involved.
3   Evidence of adaptability and willingness to learn new skills.
4   Other exam qualifications.
5   Details of referees.

Checking the advert once more, to make sure that she had not missed out any relevant details, Sandra drafted a rough letter in longhand.

Draft 1

The Personnel Officer,
Honeypot Biscuits,
Haworth Lane,
MILHAM,
Lancashire BB12 9PN.

11 Railway Street,
MILHAM,
Lancashire BB6 7TC.
15th April, 19--

Dear Sir,

I'm applying for the post of personal assistant to the managing director of Honeypot Biscuits, as advertised in the Milham Chronicle.

I recently completed a successful BTEC course at Milham College of F.E., having previously studied for a range of G.C.S.E. subjects at Milham High School. I'm nineteen years old.

Over the past three years I've had a number of part time jobs which have involved contact with the general public. For two summers I have worked at the complaints desk of the local Lowbost supermarket and have also had experience as a part time clerical assistant at Lords' Printers. In the later post I gained some basic experience of word processors and was occasionally asked to proofread copy before printing.

My typing and shorthand is up to R.S.A. 2 level and I've helped my father out with his accounts in his business as well as keeping out by serving customers in his fast food takeaway.

I believe that I'm a pretty adaptable sort of person and could quickly learn any skills required in the challenging post offered.

I'm available for interview at any time.

Yours Faithfully,

Sandra Kong

(Sandra Kong)

Sandra read through what she had written and noticed a number of technical errors as well as points where the tone or style of expression was inappropriate.

Assignment

1 List what you believe to be the technical inaccuracies in the first draft of Sandra's letter and then list any other faults you have recognized.
2 Using the same basic information, rewrite Sandra's letter as you believe it should have been rewritten in a second draft.

Comment

1 The technical inaccuracies include:
   (a) *Personel* is a misspelling of *personal*. (Sandra was getting mixed up with *personnel*)
   (b) *Successfull* is a misspelling of *successful*. (Adjectives of this type seldom have a 'full' ending)
   (c) *Later* has been used instead of *latter*. (The pronunciation is different as well as the meaning)
   (d) Faithfully should have been written faithfully, without the capital. (sincerely/faithfully/truly never have a capital when being used to conclude a letter)
2 Other faults include:
   (a) The constant abbreviation of *I'm* and *I've*. In a formal letter it is the convention to avoid these contractions. (although they are normal in everyday speech and in informal correspondence)
   (b) The opening paragraph is a statement of fact but sounds slightly impolite.
   (c) The reference to Sandra's age in the second paragraph sounds like an afterthought. Possibly it could be incorporated into the previous sentence.
   (d) The sentence which makes up the fourth paragraph contains too much information. The sentence should be split.
   (e) *Pretty* as an adjective in the fifth paragraph is slang. If an adjective is needed at all it should be a more precise one.
   (f) The six paragraphs which make up the first draft could well become five, or even four paragraphs with some advantage to clarity.
   (g) Sandra forgot to make a note of her referees.

Here is the second draft of Sandra's letter. It may well correspond closely to your rewrite.

Draft 2

The Personnel Officer,
Honeypot Biscuits,
Haworth Lane,
MILHAM,
Lancashire BB12 4PN.

11 Railway Street,
MILHAM,
Lancashire BB6 7TC,
15th April 19--

Dear Sir,

I should like to apply for the post of personal assistant as advertised in the Milham Chronicle of 13th April.

I am nineteen years of age, having recently completed a BTEC course at Milham College of F.E. While at college I successfully completed a course in shorthand and typing at R.S.A. 2 level. Prior to further education I studied for my G.C.S.E. at Milham High School. My four passes included English language and Mathematics.

In the last three years I have had a number of part time jobs, some of which have involved contact with the general public. As well as regularly helping out and serving in my father's family business I have worked for two years at the complaints and enquiry desk at the local Lowcost supermarket. I have also worked as a part time clerical assistant at Lords' Printers. While there I gained some basic experience with Amstrad word processors and was occasionally asked to proofread copy for printing.

I believe myself to be an adaptable person and have found in my brief work experience so far that I can quickly pick up new skills. I would look forward to furthering my skills in the

challenging post that is offered.

I am available for interview at short notice and include the names and addresses of two people who have agreed to act as my referees.

Yours faithfully,
Sandra Kong
(Sandra Kong)

Tracy Donaldson

SANDY BAY CORPORATION
(Department of Leisure Services)
ASSISTANT TO THE DIRECTOR OF LEISURE SERVICES

The post offered is a challenging one and involves flexible responsibilities as well as frequent contact with a wide variety of outside agencies and other departments within the corporation.

The personal qualities required are tact, imagination and patience. The qualifications required are those that will prove the applicant's competence in a wide variety of office and communication skills. Apply in writing with names and addresses of two referees to:

Giles Thomas, Staffing Officer, The Town Hall, The Promenade, SANDY BAY, Dorset SB15 7CB

Tracy Donaldson read through the advert for the sixth time. It was too good to be true. Three months' work distributing leaflets for a double glazing manufacturer had convinced her that she was not living up to her qualifications. The work was tedious, unfulfilling and very poorly paid indeed. She had only gone for it after the panic of being unemployed for five straight months after leaving college.

Tracy had been given the newspaper with the advert heavily ringed in ball pen by her father. Her family had become even more upset at Tracy's boredom as a leaflet distributor than she had herself. The advert, however, was very exciting. She needed no convincing that the job was for her, although the lack of relevant full-time experience caused her some worry.

Checking back through her records of job applications, Tracy found the CV that she had drawn up when applying for posts prior to the job with the double glazing manufacturer.

```
NAME       Tracy Donaldson

ADDRESS    80 Heathside Road
           SANDY BAY
           Dorset SB10 6AT


AGE        19

MARITAL STATUS  Single

EDUCATION  (1) Heathside County Primary School
           (2) Sandy Bay High School
           (3) Egdon College of F.E.


QUALIFICATIONS  (1) G.C.S.E. passes in six subjects (including Eng. Lang.
                    + Maths).

                (2) Preparatory module in Business Studies C.P.V.E.

                (3) Diploma of the English Speaking Board (Vocational).

                (4) R.S.A. 2 in Office Skills.

                (5) BTEC National (with Travel and Tourism option).


WORK EXPERIENCE
                (1) Two years part-time work as assistant with Cronshaw
                    Travel of Sandy Bay (5 Jan 19-- to 12 Sept 19--).

                (2) During my time at Egdon College (Sept - June) I
                    supplemented my grant by doing freelance typing for
                    students who needed their projects presenting for
                    examination.

                (3) Unpaid assistant at crèche for staff and student
                    children at Egdon College (Sept 19-- to June 19--).

                (4) Leaflet distributor (on commission basis) for
                    Security Glass Company (Nov 19-- to Feb 19--).


PRESENT POST See (4) above.

REFEREES                              (2) The Manager
(1) The Principal                         Cronshaw Travel Ltd
    Egdon College of F.E.                 Sheep Street
    Egdon Road                            SANDY BAY
    SANDY BAY                             Dorset SB3S 2TD
    Dorset SB7T 5KL
```

Assignment

1 Check the guidelines for letters of application suggested in the previous chapter.
2 Examine once more Sandra Kong's final letter of application to Honeypot Biscuits.
3 Read the Sandy Bay Leisure Services' job advertisement again.
4 Write the letter that you believe Tracy Donaldson should submit in application to Sandy Bay corporation.

You may find it useful to do a rough draft and show this to a friend who can check it through with you and spot inaccuracies of expression or suggest improvements in style or content.

You should finish by writing or typing out a polished, final draft. You could use the details contained in Tracy Donaldson's CV or, if you wish, substitute your own personal and academic details when writing this letter of application.

Comment

When writing your own *real* letter of application for a job it is a good idea to have a list of your personal, academic and work experience details handy for reference. When written down these make up your *CV* (an abbreviation for the Latin *curriculum vitae* – 'a list of your life' would be a crude translation).

The CV, together with details of the post for which you are applying, make up the raw material of your letter of application. It is up to you, as it was up to Sandra and Tracy, to make the best of your achievements in a well-organized and concise letter of application.

3 Synonyms, antonyms and euphemisms for tact and diplomacy

The above heading is full of rather frightening sounding words. As is so often the case, the words themselves have fairly simple meanings and are only shorter ways of expressing ideas that would take longer to express otherwise.

A *synonym* is a word that has a similar meaning to another word and which may be substituted for it in a sentence without affecting the overall meaning, eg:

The man was a *famous* actor.

The man was an *eminent* actor.

('Famous' and 'eminent' are synonyms.)

An *antonym* is a word of opposite meaning, eg:

The weather was *hot* for the time of year.

The weather was *cold* for the time of year.

('Hot' and 'cold' are antonyms and their use completely changes the meaning of a sentence.)

A *euphemism* is a mild or more polite word or phrase that is used for a harsh or unpleasant word or phrase, eg:

His aunt had *died*.

His aunt had *passed away*.

Tack and diplomacy are skills that permit difficult negotiations to be completed without ill feeling. These are obviously skills that are useful in one's personal as well as working life.

Consider the following two reports on somebody:

Report 1

'Tony is chronically unpunctual as well as being a nuisance in class. He has an atrocious record of absence and is a born troublemaker in the few classes he does attend. He is rude to staff and his written work is disgustingly sloppy on the very rare occasions he does complete his homework.'

Report 2

'Tony's punctuality and attendance are a source of grave concern to his teachers. His behaviour to staff and fellow students when he does attend class leaves much to be desired. His written work, which is seldom completed, displays consistent technical inaccuracies.'

You will realize, on reading the two reports on Tony, that the facts have not been changed. Each report comments on Tony's poor punctuality and attendance, behaviour to staff and students, standard and insufficiency of written work. The difference between the two reports lies in the manner in which the opinions are expressed.

Whichever report is actually presented to Tony or his parents there is no escaping from the fact that Tony is in trouble.

However, the first report verges on the abusive and is more likely to antagonize Tony and his family than lead to a positive discussion of problems.

You may like to read through the two reports again and isolate the words and phrases that make the second report more diplomatic. These words and phrases will probably be synonyms or euphemisms.

Tactful use of synonyms or euphemisms

The reasons for this are:
1   To avoid ill-feeling which would result in a negative response.
2   To retain working relations with the party concerned.
3   To retain personal dignity without sinking to abuse.
4   To avoid possible changes of libel or slander.
5   To avoid tedious repetition where a particular word or phrase has to be repeated.

Exercise

Here is a list of words for each of which a number of synonyms exists. Write down as many synonyms as you can find for each word in the list. You may find it helpful to mentally put each original word into a sentence and think of the synonyms you could use, eg:

BEAUTIFUL   gorgeous, pretty, handsome, fine, sublime, exquisite, radiant, graceful, lovely, blooming.

(You will realize that the use of the above synonyms would depend upon whether you were describing a woman, a sunset or a vase!)

PROSPEROUS   –
TIRED   –
ARGUE   –
LAZY   –
DIFFICULT   –
CHEAP   –
FEAR   –
NICE   –
BIG   –
SMALL   –

The point of recognizing the synonyms, antonyms and euphemisms that exist as alternative to individual words is more than simply an academic one. There is no point in 'expanding your word-power' simply for the sake of it. It is only useful to know a word's alternatives if the use of the alternative leads to greater success in the communication of one's ideas or opinions.

An area of work where words are particularly important in communication and persuasion is the law. Lawyers and barristers arguing for the prosecution or defence have nothing but words with which to persuade judge and jury to their point of view.

Example 1

'Ladies and gentlemen of the jury, we on the prosecution side will hope to prove to you that the accused is a menace to society. After driving at a ridiculously high speed through rush hour traffic in a manner that can only be described as reckless, the accused committed a grievous assault on a CID officer who apprehended him at the site of the horrifying crash at the end of the High Street. The fullest penalty of which the law is capable should be imposed on this man who is a menace to society as well as suicidal in his totally irresponsible driving.'

The above introductory remarks by the prosecuting counsel attempt to use words in an emotive and persuasive manner. It may seem that there is no more to be said and that the accused is heading for a severe fine and loss of his licence, if not worse. The counsel for the defence, however, may well describe the same events in the following words.

Example 2

'Ladies and gentlemen of the jury, we on the defence side will hope to prove that the accused is a victim of circumstance. Being a stranger to the town the accused was not familiar with the speed limit that was in operation at the time in question. You may imagine his distress when, after writing off his car at the accident black spot at the end of the High Street, my client was approached aggressively by a man who he quite naturally assumed was an ordinary pedestrian. It was only after the confused scuffle on the pavement that the accused realized that the pedestrian was a plain-clothes policeman. We hope that you will deal leniently with this unfortunate man who has inadvertently found himself in contravention of the law.'

Exercise

The same incidents are dealt with but the language used by each speaker differs in order to give the listener a different slant on the events. You could examine each example to discover the words and phrases that are used to gain such a different effect, eg:

'The accused is a menace to society.' (Example 1)
'The accused is a victim of circumstance.' (Example 2)

You may have found that the defence counsel in his remarks tended to use euphemisms. There are many areas of work where euphemisms are used frequently.

People whose job it is to sell holidays are frequent users of euphemism.

Exercise

Use your imagination to decide what are the harsher facts that could lie behind the euphemisms used in the following extract from a holiday brochure.

'The Hotel El Plonko is within *easy walking distance* of the *popular* beach and is situated *close to the shops* and bars of Los Plonkos. *Compact studio accommodation* is available as well as luxurious single rooms with *en suite facilities*. The *busy* restaurant is famed for its *international cuisine* and the disco is *particularly favoured* by the youth of the district. The *liveliness* of the bar and the proximity to the *commercial port area* make the Hotel El Plonko *less suitable* for family holidays.'

As you may have realized by now the difference between a euphemism and a lie is often difficult to distinguish. It is when the gap between the hard reality and the euphemism becomes stretched too far that we can substitute the word 'lie' for 'euphemism'.

Just as opinions may differ concerning fact and euphemism, it is in the extreme differences of opinion that the *antonym* comes into its own. When two parties are in total disagreement they will deny each other's statements and opinions by the use of antonyms. Here is an example of a review that might have been written about a popular TV 'soap'.

Example 1

'Last night's edition of 'Dallas' *soared* to new *heights* of *cleverness*. There is so *much* to admire in this dramatic presentation but we all watch it for different reasons. *Interesting* fashions and *tasteful* interior decorations amuse some viewers but others switch on to experience the sheer *liveliness* of the acting. *Occasional* background music accompanies the *exterior* scenes and ultimately everyone is forced to acknowledge the *reality* of the situations and the *inspiring* nature of the themes presented.'

The use of antonyms would allow a less sympathetic reviewer of this international TV offering to write the review as follows:

Example 2

'Last night's edition of 'Dallas' *plummeted* to new *depths* of *stupidity*. There is so *little* to admire in this dramatic presentation but we all watch it for different reasons. *Boring* fashions and *tasteless* interior decorations amuse some viewers but others switch on to experience the sheer *boredom* of the acting. *Incessant* background music accompanies the *interior* scenes and ultimately everyone is forced to acknowledge the *fantasy* of the situations and the *uninspiring* nature of the themes presented.'

You will recognize that the antonyms that totally change the reviews of 'Dallas' are formed by:

1 changing the prefix of the original word, eg 'inspiring' becomes '*un*inspiring'; *or*
2 changing the suffix of the original work, eg 'tasteful' becomes 'taste*less*'; *or*
3 changing the original word entirely, eg 'soared' becomes 'plummeted'.

Exercise

For each underlined word in the following sentences provide (a) a synonym and (b) an antonym that could be used in the sentence without altering its structure, eg:

The *clever* student gained the result she deserved.
(a) synonym *intelligent* (b) antonym *foolish*

1 He *grinned* at his mother as she scolded him.

2   The *rise* in government spending was unexpected.
3   He had a *minor* operation in hospital.
4   The *wealthy* woman was careful with her money.
5   The missing object was *hidden* by my sister.
6   The term *begins* next week.
7   She spoke *aggressively* to the child.
8   There was an *entertaining* demonstration of tap dancing.
9   A *large* crowd gathered outside the gates.
10 They drove at *increased* speed as they neared the port.

Here is a description of a house and its situation as it might be honestly outlined by a surveyor. It attempts to make an unbiased summary of the essential facts.

'The property is situated on a very busy road that carries heavy traffic to the newly built motorway extension. It has very small garden areas and the property backs on to a supermarket car park. It has only one bedroom and the bathroom, kitchen and lounge are in desperate need of redecoration. An open fire in the lounge runs one radiator and the house is generally cold with some traces of damp in upstairs rooms. There are a number of Victorian features that a new owner would need to strip out in order to make the house habitable, eg a stone sink in the kitchen, a stained cast iron bath and a wooden staircase with traces of woodworm that leads to the attic.'

Exercise

Imagine yourself to be an estate agent with the unenviable task of selling the above house. Using euphemisms and antonyms and whatever other techniques you believe to be useful, rewrite the above paragraph, sentence by sentence, in such a way as to make the property appear to be 'a desirable residence'. (You may find it useful to read some estate agents' house descriptions in your local paper.)

The first sentence of the surveyor's report might be rewritten as: 'The property is within easy access of the motorway for buyers wishing to commute.'

English in use

Subject and verb agreement

It is necessary for a sentence to have a subject and a verb in order to be acceptable grammatically. Usually a sentence contains more than the subject and the verb and this is what can cause confusion. No matter how many words a sentence contains it should always be remembered that:

1 A *subject* that is *singular* must have a *verb* that is *singular*.
2 A *subject* that is *plural* must have a *verb* that is *plural*.

> For example:
> *One* of the students *is* gaining dangerously low marks. (Singular subject with singular verb.)
> The *wheels* of the car *are* to be examined for faults. (Plural subject with plural verb.)

The more words there are between subject and verb the more likely there is to be error in subject/verb agreement. Even in the above examples it is important to recognize which is the subject of each sentence.

> In example 1 the subject is not 'students' but 'One' of the students and, therefore, the verb is singular.
> In example 2 the subject is not 'car' but 'wheels' and, therefore, the verb is plural.
> It is a so-called general 'rule' that collective nouns count as singular for verb agreement and, although this is generally true, one should be aware of a variation in the rule. If individuals or parts of the collective noun act individually then the verb has to be in the plural, eg:

1 The class *was* able to finish the exam in the time allowed. (The class as a collective group controls the verb as singular.)
2 The class *were* divided in their ability to complete the exam. (Individuals within the collective group control the verb as plural.)

The use of 'shall' and 'will'

There is great carelessness in the way speakers and writers use 'shall' and 'will' as if they were acceptable alternatives, no matter what the circumstances. There are some fairly simple formulae for deciding when to use 'shall' or 'will'.

1 *when making a simple statement in the future tense use*
I *shall*
You will
He/She/It will
We *shall*
They will

> For example
> I *shall* go for a walk this afternoon.
> It *will* be a difficult decision.

2   *If you wish to express determination of intention the reverse of the above formula applies*
   I *will*
   You shall
   He/She/It shall
   We *will*
   They shall

For example:
   I *will* not tolerate your insolence a moment longer.
      You *shall* do your homework even if I have to stand over you.

'Sincerely' and 'faithfully'

Some confusion seems to arise when deciding whether to use *sincerely* or *faithfully* before signing off at the conclusion of a letter. There is really no need to be confused as the accepted practice is quite easy to remember once it has been outlined clearly.

1   'Yours *sincerely*' is only used when the opening of the letter consists of a named individual, eg Dear Mrs Taylor/Dear Mr Jackson/Dear Ms Norton/Dear John, etc.
2   'Yours *faithfully*' is used when the opening of the letter does *not* contain the personal name of the individual to whom it is addressed, eg Dear Sir/Dear Sirs/Dear Madam/Dear Managing Director, etc.

Exercise (subject/verb agreement)

Fill in the blanks in the following sentences with the singular or plural of the verb suggested.
1   We .(to hope). that the test is an easy one.
2   She never .(to go). to the shops on Saturday.
3   Some of the workers .(to be). on strike.
4   The herd of cattle .(to be). scattered in different parts of the farm.
5   The herd of cattle .(to be). safely in the field.

Exercise (use of 'shall'/'will')

Fill in the blanks in the following sentences with 'will' or 'shall' as appropriate.

1   We .... go on a picnic tomorrow if it is fine.
2   They .... not pass their exams without some effort.
3   You .... only open that door over my dead body!
4   We .... move heaven and earth to reach the summit.
5   It .... probably be raining tomorrow.

4 Ongoing case studies

Honeypot Biscuits

Sandra Kong had recovered from her astonishment at the success of her interview. Having spent the last of her small savings on a neat and efficient outfit to wear for work, Sandra arrived at Honeypot Biscuits for her first day's work.

After being shown round the different departments and introduced to the workers and various section supervisors, Mrs Jarvis showed her into her small office. It was situated immediately next to her own and contained a desk, filing cabinets, typewriter, spirit duplicator, desk top photocopier and two telephones. It all seemed very impressive to Sandra and she still wondered how her interview had gone so well.

'Sandra, we'll discuss the day-to-day routine this afternoon. For now there's a busy morning ahead of you. You may recall that there were eight other candidates for your post on the day of the interview and they all need a tactful letter of apology. There's also a list of 30 other applicants who didn't get as far as an interview.'

'I'm sorry, but what do you mean by "apology" Mrs Jarvis?'

'Our apology that we could not offer them a post at this time. Wish them luck with their future applications – that sort of thing.'

'I see.'

'Be diplomatic. We're an expanding company and might be able to take on some more clerical staff in the future. I'll send you a list of their names and addresses. We could do with two sets of letters; one for the applicants we interviewed and another for the ones that weren't invited.'

Sandra sat at her desk and reached for a notepad to draft out the two letters that Mrs Jarvis required. For the general letter that was to be sent out to the 30 applicants who failed to get an interview she drafted the following:

```
A N Other
1 Any Street
Milham
Lancs
BB11 8TY

Dear .........
        We should like to thank you for your application for the post of
personal assistant with this company.  We had an awful lot of
applications and found it almost impossible to make a shortlist.

        Interviews have now taken place however and an appointment has been
made.  We're very sorry to have to say that you have failed in this
instance.

        We should like to thank you once again for your application and
wish you better luck in the future.

                        Yours faithfully



                (Angela Jarvis - Managing Director)
```

Tracy read through the first draft and found a number of points that were unsatisfactory. She was happy enough with the overall structure but was critical of the following:

1   . . . an awful lot of applications . . .
2   . . . almost impossible . . .
3   . . . very sorry to say . . .
4   . . . failed . . .
5   . . . wish you better luck . . .

Exercise

Remembering what was said in the previous chapter about synonyms, antonyms and euphemisms, supply more businesslike and precise expressions for each of the above words or phrases.

Comment

There are a number of possibilities for improving the above words or phrases. Here is the second draft of the general letter, containing Sandra Kong's improvements.

```
A N Other
1 Any Street
MILHAM
Lancs
BB1 8TY

Dear .........

     We should like to thank you for your recent application for the
post of personal assistant with this company.  We received a large
number of enquiries which made the selection of candidates for interview
extremely difficult.

     Interviews have now taken place and an appointment has been made.
We regret to say that in this instance your application has been
unsuccessful.

     We thank you once again for your interest in this company and wish
you success in your future career.

                    Yours faithfully



          (Angela Jarvis - Managing Director)
```

The letter was approved by Mrs Jarvis and Sandra turned her attention to the second letter. This was the one that was to be sent to the applicants who were not appointed on the day of the interviews. At first she found this a very difficult task as she had met all the names on the list. However, Sandra soon settled down, to write a slightly different 'letter of rejection' for the eight shortlisted candidates. She was aware, that having got so close to appointment, the candidates would require a particularly tactful letter.

Sandra also remembered that the company was still expanding and might want to appoint more clerical staff in the future. She realized that it would be desirable to keep the goodwill of these rejected applicants as they might be useful to approach in the months to come.

Assignment

Bearing in mind that the recipient of each letter was considered sufficiently qualified to have been interviewed for the post, draft the letter you believe Sandra should write. Remember that the recipients may be useful to Honeypot Biscuits in the future.

Sandy Bay Leisure Services

Tracy Donaldson looked at the office in dismay. It was tiny, poorly decorated and in a state of chaos. Files, letters and stationery were scattered over shelves, the desk and the floor. She realized now why Mr Bickerstaffe had stressed at the interview that he wanted someone who could use their initiative as well as follow instructions. It would certainly take some initiative as well as hard manual labour to make her office look better than an untidy store cupboard.

Most of the morning had gone by and Tracy was looking slightly worn when Mr Bickerstaffe popped his head round the door.

'Well, I must say you've worked miracles here! It really does look like an office at last. Well done Tracy.'

She looked round at the efficiently stacked paperwork, twin filing cabinets, telephone and intercom and typewriter. It looked as if one could at least try to be efficient in such a working environment.

'Thanks Mr Bickerstaffe. There doesn't seem to be any reprographic equipment though.'

'Reprographic equipment?'

'Duplicator or photocopier, Mr Bickerstaffe.'

He laughed.

'You'll have to use the photocopier in the general office. We can't have one of our own or the rate payers would go mad. Perhaps next year if I can keep the advertising budget down.'

'It would be very useful Mr Bickerstaffe.'

'We'll see. For now I've got a rather delicate job for you.

It needs to be done by lunchtime I'm afraid. I got one of the office girls to get a rejection letter out to the candidates who failed to get your job. They all went out yesterday. Since then we've realized that one of the girls we interviewed would be O.K. for an assistant to my colleague Jack Trevor in the General Duties section. His secretary, Sandra Ames, has handed in her notice suddenly and there's this unexpected vacancy.

'Josephine Hindle is the candidate we'd like to ask back for an informal interview but she's not going to be in a very good mood having been rejected by us once.

'Drop her an apologetic note and ask her if she would like to contact Jack Trevor quickly to discuss the possibility of her taking over Sandra's job. Try not to make us seem too disorganized. I'll have a glance at the letter before I go off for lunch.'

Assignment

Tracy found Miss Hindle's details and address on file. She is living with her aunt at 80 Cliff Road, Sandy Bay, Dorset SB7 2AX. Write the tactful letter that Tracy has been instructed to draft. Remember that you must:

1 Cover up the administrative confusion apparently displayed by Sandy Bay Leisure Services.
2 Explain why the post is now available, without going into excessive detail.
3 Ask Miss Hindle to contact Mr Trevor to arrange an early meeting.
4 Avoid suggesting that the post available is 'second best'. (The Sandy Bay Leisure Services address is to be found in Chapter 2.)

5 Models for organization and communication within a variety of institutions

A self-employed person who manufactures a product or provides a service does not need a model in order to understand his or her position within a system. A self-employed person has only to communicate with his, or her, customers and possibly suppliers. It is most unlikely that the scale of a single person's business operation would require a model to assist communication.

The majority of us, however, work within an institution of small, medium or large scale. In order for us to understand how we fit into the system and in order to communication by the best route with others in the system we need some sort of model. Once we recognize our place in the model, communication is eased with the three groups with which we share the system:

1 Those who work in a *superior* position to ourselves.
2 Those who work as *equals* to ourselves.
3 Those who work in a *lower* position to ourselves.

If we take as an example a medium-scale shop that specializes in high-quality dairy products and cooked meats we may find the simple 'tree' model as shown in Figure 5.1.

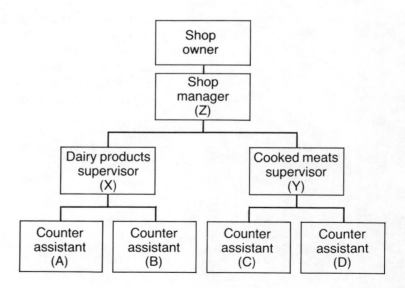

Figure 5.1   Tree model of hierarchy

In the case of an institution as small as this kind of retail outlet there is no real need for a model as it will be quite clear to the seven people who work for the owner where they stand in relation to each other.

The supervisors (X) and (Y) are of equal status and know that they are responsible to the overall manager (Z).

Counter assistants (A) and (B) know that they are immediately responsible to (X).

Counter assistants (C) and (D) know that they are immediately responsible to (Y).

(A), (B), (C) and (D) know that they are of equal status.

It is unlikely that in such a scale of institution people will work in absolute isolation, but in order to maintain good working relationships the model allows each person in the system to find answers to the following questions:

1   What are the limits of my responsibility?
2   To whom am I answerable?
3   To whom do I turn for advice?
4   For whom am I responsible?

There are different ways of presenting models of organization. Generally speaking, the larger the organization, the more complex is the model. It is, however, in larger organizations that workers have most need of understanding where they are in the system.

If you are a student taking a course at a school or college, you may be aware of the size of the institution. Apart from the lecturers or teachers you may be aware of others who allow the organization to keep operating. There is probably a canteen where you can get a drink or a meal. You will have noticed a general office or enquiry desk where fees are paid and administrative problems resolved. You may not have thought about the maintenance and caretaking staff who attempt to keep the building clean, lit and heated. In other words there are catering staff, administrative staff and maintenance staff in addition to the teaching staff.

Wheel

Figure 5.2 is a 'wheel' model that depicts the possible organization of a medium-sized college. This model allows one to discover the organization and division of teaching and non-teaching staff.

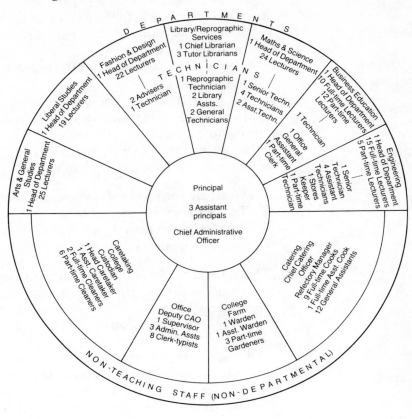

Figure 5.2   Wheel

Daisy loop

Another way of portraying routes or networks of communication within an organization is the daisy loop shown in Figure 5.3.

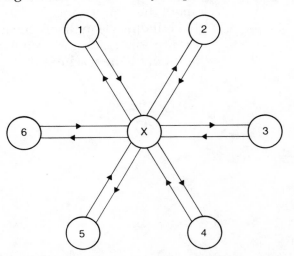

Figure 5.3   Daisy loop

In this model the manager or chief executive X is allowed a flow of information/communication to and from the sections or departments 1 to 6. The model does not show communication between the six sections and departments.

Simple loop

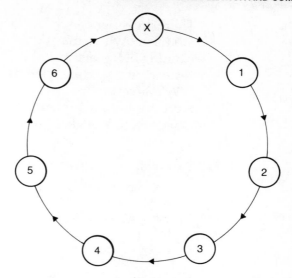

Figure 5.4   Simple loop

In this model (Figure 5.4) communication to and from executive X goes via the different sections or departments in the organization. No model can make full allowance for all the routes by which communication takes place within a system. There are all sorts of unofficial routes by which rumour and word of mouth allow facts and opinions to be circulated. Any model that attempted to depict all such routes would be virtually impossible to design and equally impossible to interpret.

Possible 'star' model

This model illustrates the central position of an office within a manufacturing or service organization (Figure 5.5).

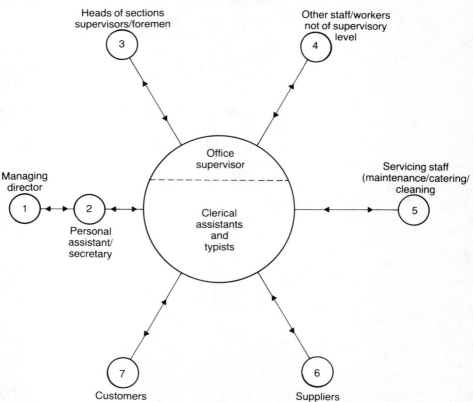

Figure 5.5   Star model

There are other combinations of staff which are outside this model but which may be very important to the smooth and fair running of the organization. These might include trade unions, social clubs, staff associations, etc.

Whatever a person's position or placing in the model or system there are certain demands that will, quite rightly, be made upon that person. Whether one is managing director or counter assistant the following criteria of behaviour may be expected:

1 Loyalty to colleagues in the organization.
2 Tasks completed to the best of one's ability.
3 Information received is promptly acted upon and passed on if necessary.
4 Initiative displayed when faced with difficulty.
5 Cooperation with fellow members of the organization.

Understanding the model of your institution and your place within it enables you to work *efficiently* and *harmoniously*. Communication can pass smoothly to you and you can communicate in return with relative ease when you understand the 'map' upon which you have a place.

Assignment

Fulfil either 1 *or* 2 below.
1 If you are a full-time student at a school or college, try to draw a model of the organization. You will need to talk to staff or members of the administration. The college handbook may be helpful. Find out how the courses and staff are divided between the different departments. Use whichever type of model you feel most appropriate (tree, wheel, daisy loop, simple loop, star).
2 If you are a part-time student or find difficulty in obtaining information from a school or college, try talking to the administrative staff of a supermarket, department store, large library, to see if you can devise a model for such an institution.

Whichever assignment you choose to undertake, be patient, be diplomatic and ask lots of questions. It would be both courteous and useful to show the model you design to someone who has helped you with advice. See if he or she believes your model to be an accurate portrayal of the organization.

6 Ongoing case studies

Sandy Bay Leisure Services

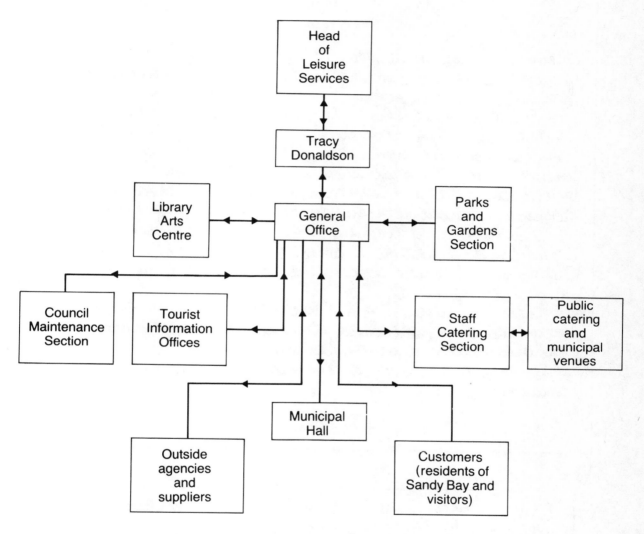

Figure 6.1   Structure of Sandy Bay Leisure Services

Tracy Donaldson examined the model she had sketched out.
From talking to the supervisor of the general office and checking
with Mr Bickerstaffe she was reasonably satisfied that the model
was an accurate portrayal of the structure of Sandy Bay Leisure
Services. She was relieved that she had persevered in getting the
different sections of the organization sorted out into a plan
(Figure 6.1). Mr Bickerstaffe's latest request, that lay in memo
form on her desk, made the model an essential part of the speedy
completion of her task.

INTERNAL OFFICE MEMORANDUM

TO *Tracy Donaldson*

FROM *A. Bickerstaffe*

REF *AB*

DATE *14 Oct 19--*

SUBJECT *Punctuality*

I am most concerned about the standard of punctuality for arrival at work on the part of certain members of the Leisure Services staff.

I notice on checking the copies of salary pay dockets that approximately 20 per cent of the department were late for work more than three times during the last month. I realize that there are some circumstances that make the odd late arrival for work inevitable but these 20 per cent need a reminder of their working hours.

I would only lose my temper if I approached them directly. I don't want to send out a reminder to the whole staff as the 80 per cent who are punctual might be offended.

Please draft a firm but tactful memo to the members concerned and let the office supervisor know to which departments they should be distributed. A list of the relevant staff is attached.

AB

Leisure Services staff with three or more late arrivals at work in the last month of paid salary

J Allinson - Schools Liason Assistant at the Library Centre
A Carter - Trainee Gardener in Memorial Park
S B Dawney - Electrician
F Everett - Counter assistant at Information Centre
D Moon - Driver for Parks Department
M Starkey - Cleaner
M Thompson - Typist
J Varley - Kitchen assistant

AB

Assignment

You will find information and advice on the layout of memoranda in the following chapter. Without worrying too much at this stage about the layout at the head of the memo, draft the 'firm but tactful' message that Mr Bickerstaffe requires Tracy to write. You should also list the departments that need to be sent copies of the memo.

Comment

You should compare the messages you have composed with those written by other members of your group. Discuss whether the correct balance between *firmness* and *tactfulness* has been achieved. With the help of Tracy's model for the Leisure Services Department, you should have listed the following departments as needing copies of the memo:

1 Library Arts Centre – J Allinson
2 Parks and Gardens – A Carter and D Moon
3 Council Maintenance – S B Downey
4 Tourist Information Office – F Everett and N Starkey
5 General Office – M Thompson
6 Catering Section – T Varley

With the appropriate memo and the above list, the general office will be able to ensure that the communication of Mr Bickerstaffe's displeasure over lack of punctuality is speedily passed on to those it concerns, without others being affected.

Honeypot Biscuits

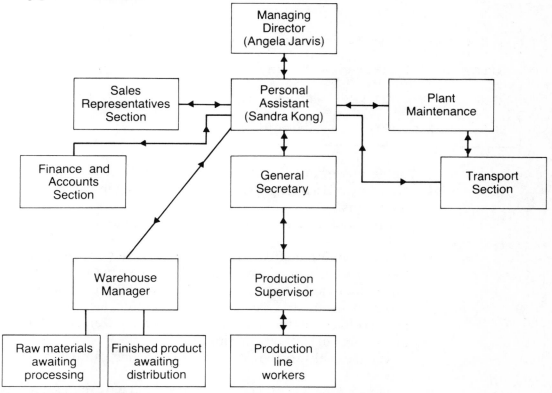

Figure 6.2   Structure of Honeypot Biscuits

Sandra Kong studied the model that Mrs Jarvis had given her to explain the organization of Honeypot Biscuits and her place within it. At first glance it had looked confusing but as she had familiarized herself with the company during the first few days of work, she began to realize that it was very helpful.

Mrs Jarvis had also provided her with a staff list of the complete company.

```
                     HONEYPOT BISCUITS

MANAGING DIRECTOR       - Angela Jarvis

PLANT MAINTENANCE       - Tony Craig (production line)
                          Arthur Owen (transport)

TRANSPORT SECTION       - Giles Ellis, Peter Frazer, Stanley Morton,
                          Ralph Owen (delivery van drivers)
                          Peter Collins, Raymond Heath
                          (fork lift truck drivers)

PRODUCTION SUPERVISOR   - Catherine Cooper

PRODUCTION WORKERS      - Tony Cooper, Claire Frazer, Sandra Limmer,
                          Joyce MacSween, Celia Martin, Joy Nutter,
                          Agnes Pitt, Mark Riley, Tracy Slade,
                          Gill Taylor

WAREHOUSE MANAGER       - Trevor Lee

WAREHOUSE ASSISTANT     - Tony Dronsfield

FINANCE AND ACCOUNTS    - Alan Botham (acting personnel officer)

ACCOUNTS ASSISTANT      - Charles Jarvis

SALES REPRESENTATIVES   - Stephen Daldry, Mary Hughes, David Moor

GENERAL SECRETARY       - Karen Warner
```

'Sandra, I've had a circular from the local police headquarters. They've initiated a campaign for safer driving in winter conditions.'

'That sounds like a good idea Mrs Jarvis, but how does it affect us?'

'Well Sandra, it affects us in two ways. We've got employees on the staff whose job is driving and then we've got those who drive cars in their non-working hours. Honeypot Biscuits can only benefit if all our staff are made aware of safety factors. We'll have fewer vehicles off the road in winter for repairs and a reduction in the number of staff off with injuries.'

'What exactly are the police offering in their campaign, Mrs Jarvis?'

'Here's their leaflet. Have a look at it and we can discuss ways of contacting the right staff this afternoon.'

DON'T BE A WALLY IN WINTER WEATHER!

DRIVERS . . . Do you know what to do when braking on wet or icy roads?
Do you know how to control a skid?
Do you know how to get your vehicle going again when it is stopped by snow?

Milham Constabulary are concerned at the dangers to which drivers are exposing both themselves and other road users when taking their vehicles out in wintry conditions.

WHAT CAN WE DO FOR YOU?

An experienced police instructor can come and give an illustrated lecture at your place of work if the management agrees. Whether you drive for a living or drive for domestic purposes, we have something to offer you. As a follow-up we can offer an hour's free, practical tuition on the police skid pan for those who wish to avail themselves of really useful safety instruction.

Contact us for further details at:
Milham Police Station, High Street, MILHAM, Lancs. BB3 7QT

Sandra read the leaflet from Milham police once more and then examined the model and personnel list of Honeypot Biscuits. Since she had no way of knowing who used a car for domestic purposes she concentrated on isolating the staff who drove professionally for the company.

Exercise

1 Which departments or sections of Honeypot Biscuits contain professional drivers who need to be contacted with a memo concerning the Milham police offer?
2 List the individuals within the above departments who need to be contacted with any memo that might be circulated to these departments.

Comment

The question of which departments or sections need to be contacted is fairly easy to settle. The Transport Section with its delivery van drivers (and possibly fork lift truck drivers) needs to be contacted as well as the Sales Representatives Section.

The individuals within the *Transport* Section are Peter Collins, Giles Ellis, Peter Frazer, Raymond Heath, Stanley Morton and Ralph Owen.

The individuals within the *Sales Representatives* Section who need contacting are Stephen Daldry, Mary Hughes and David Moor.

In later conversation with Mrs Jarvis it was decided that Sandra should send a photocopy of the Milham police leaflet to all personnel except the individuals in the Transport and Sales Sections. These 'professional' drivers were to be contacted by a diplomatic memo.

'Some of them have been driving for years Sandra,' said Mrs Jarvis, 'and they might be rather sensitive about suggesting that they could improve their driving. We've got a good record so far and the only incidents in the last two years have been a speeding offence and a parking fine for one of the delivery drivers. It would be silly to miss out on this opportunity however.

'Let our drivers know they can have paid time off work to attend a session on the skid pan. We'll have the lecture during work time as well. I don't want to force them to volunteer but I *do* want them to take advantage of the offer. I'll have a look at your memo when you've drafted it.'

Assignment

Without worrying about the layout of the memorandum at this stage, draft the body of the required message. You should remember that offence to possibly experienced drivers should be avoided but firm persuasion to volunteer be evident.

7 The design and writing of a memorandum

Memorandum–memoranda–memo – all these words are used, somewhat confusingly it may seem, to refer to a particular form of internal communication. Strictly speaking, *memorandum* is the singular form of the word and is used when talking of a single internal communication. *Memoranda* is the plural and would be used when referring to a number of internal communications. *Memo* and *memos* are abbreviations of the singular and plural and are most commonly used in the world of work.

The precise meaning of memorandum is 'something that is used to remind', although the term has come to be used in business as 'something that is used to draw someone else's attention to a certain matter'.

Very often an institution will use a ready printed form on which the staff will write their messages or it may be that individuals have to design their own forms each time they write a message. Whichever procedure operates, the following should be clearly indicated:

1 For whom the message is intended.
2 Who has sent the message.
3 When the message was written.
4 What is the basic content of the message.

Although the above may seem rather formal, it is necessary to be organized when communication is taking place within an institution that has a complex organization. You may recall some of the more complicated models illustrated in the previous two chapters. In a network that is large and with many departments some form of common system of internal communication is highly desirable for reasons of speed and clarity.

A typical blank memo form might appear as follows:

INTERNAL OFFICE MEMORANDUM

TO ....   REF ....

FROM ....   DATE ....

SUBJECT ....

The advantages of this commonly accepted format are:

1   The reasonably limited space in the body of the form forces the writer of the memo to be concise.
2   The recipient of the form recognizes the source and subject matter quickly.
3   The writer automatically fills in the relevant information in the appropriate spaces on the form.
4   The form makes it easy for an office or internal communications service to recognize the intended recipient.

Although the memo has some relationship to a report in that it allows one person's opinions or thoughts to be transmitted to another person, it differs in the important essential that it is not requested and, therefore, has completely open terms of reference. A report is always requested and the writer of a report must always limit his or her response to the terms of reference set by the person who requested the report. (See Chapters 17 and 18 on report writing.)

The sender and receiver, who are indicated in the TO and FROM spaces at the head of the memo, are referred to by:

1   their titles in the organization, eg Managing Director, Officer Supervisor, Sales Representative; or
2   their personal names, eg Alice Barkham, Anthony Henshaw. (titles such as Mrs/Ms/Mr are not used).

In the rare case of a memo conveying a lengthy or complex idea, the use of subheadings is customary. This allows the recipient to comprehend the message more quickly. This is seldom necessary, however, as the essence of a memo is usually its conciseness and brevity.

The tone of the memo

Although a memo is used to communicate within an organization (in which it is quite possible that all the personnel are known to each other), it is important that an appropriate tone is adopted when drafting the message.

You will recall that a previous chapter pointed out that commonsense analysis of an institutional model showed it to be made up of personnel who are one's superiors, subordinates or equals. Whichever group the receiver of the memo belongs in, it is important to be aware of that person's feelings.

It is bad communication to indulge in casual familiarity or arrogant rudeness when using the memo. Whether one is communicating with senior management or a subordinate within the structure, an appropriate tone should be adopted. This tone will be slightly adjusted by the writer dependent upon: familiarity with the receiver of the message; and the content of the message.

In considering the *receiver* of the message and the tone to be adopted, the following factors may be relevant:

1   Is the receiver one's superior in the organization?
2   Is the receiver one's subordinate – possibly new to the organization and inexperienced?
3   Is the receiver likely to understand the message if it is of specialized or complex nature?
4   Is the receiver in a different department and possibly without experience or knowledge of the matter to which reference is being made?
5   Are copies of the memo going to be read by others in the system?

In considering the *content* of the message, the following factors may be relevant:

1   Is the content factual and specific with the intention of supplying new information? (If this is the case the message should be logically structured with precise vocabulary and no chance of ambiguous interpretation.)
2   Is the content attempting to persuade the receiver to agree with writer's opinions and possibly alter his attitude and working habits? (If this is the case then persuasive words and phrases should be adopted that will avoid an adverse reaction on the part of the receiver and encourage a positive response.)
3   Is the content requesting information or help? (If this is the case then some care should be taken in adopting an appropriate tone as was suggested in 2 above.)

Exercise

Consider the following messages from memoranda. Imagine yourself to have been the receiver. Which messages do you feel have adopted a tone that would be acceptable to you and likely to stimulate a willing response?

1   We're going to have to cut down on wasteful use of electricity in your department. Don't use the lights during the daytime or else there'll be trouble. Of course, if it's a dark day and lack of lighting might cause danger or interference with efficiency then I suppose the lights will have to be switched on. I want some cooperation in this matter.
2   I hear you've been turning up for work late. This just isn't on. Most of the others in your section manage to get here on time so why can't you?
3   Commencing Monday morning 16 July 19-- the staff car park will be marked out with numbered spaces. This is to avoid the haphazard parking that has been developing recently and to ensure that a space is available for all personnel. A list of the numbers that have been allocated to staff is attached. I hope that you will cooperate in this scheme and trust that you will inform me of any problems that may arise.

Comment

It would be surprising if you had accepted the first two as appropriate in tone and sufficiently tactful to earn a positive response.

Memo 1 is vague. No definition is made of 'wasteful' or 'trouble'. There is no attempt to adopt a persuasive or reasonable tone. The only likely result of such a memo is either confusion or ill-feeling.

Memo 2 is insulting and imprecise. Although the receiver probably has been unpunctual, he or she is unlikely to be persuaded by such a curt message. Is the receiver genuinely supposed to answer the question at the end? The sender of the memo has shown neither concern for the receiver's feelings nor considered the likelihood of the memo's power to persuade.

Memo 3 is reasonably clear, precise in its detail and helpful in its final request for any problems to be transmitted back through the system.

As an addition to this exercise you might like to rewrite the first two messages (using some imagination to supply added information where you feel appropriate) in such a way as will take into account the receiver and the purpose of the message.

8 Ongoing case studies

Honeypot Biscuits

'Look Sandra, this has got to be sorted out. I've just come back from a meeting at the bank and had to park my car out on the road near the entrance.'

'The car park *is* rather full, Mrs Jarvis. I suppose it's because it's Friday.'

'What's Friday to do with anything?'

'Well, the staff get paid today and some of the husbands meet their wives out of work so that they can go straight on to the supermarket.'

'Oh very nice! The managing director has to park out in the road and get soaked into the bargain.'

'There's a delivery of packaging materials due in half an hour by Westerman's truck, as well.'

'That's all we need. We'll try and sort it out for today by getting the sales reps to move their cars into the maintenance bay so that Westerman's truck can get in, but we've got to sort out a better system.'

'What had you got in mind Mrs Jarvis?'

'The simplest thing is to ensure that the only vehicles using the car park are Honeypot Biscuit vehicles or cars used by employees for transport to work. That should ensure that our limited space isn't used as a short stay car park by all and sundry, even if they are relatives of workers. Get a memo out to all the staff, Sandra. We may by able to extend the car park next spring, but for now it must be no temporary parking. See they understand I'm serious about this. It's interfering with the smooth running of the business . . . and my shoes are wet!'

Sandra first of all listed the relevant points that would need to be included in the memo she was required to draft for Mrs Jarvis.

Exercise 1

List the information that Sandra should include in the memo.

Comment 1

Having decided what should be included or left out, you should have been left with something close to the following items in your preparatory list.

1. The Honeypot Biscuits car park is of limited capacity.
2. The car park must only be used for Honeypot Biscuits vehicles (reps' cars and delivery trucks) or personal transport used by employees for transport to work.
3. Possibility of car park being extended next year.
4. Delivery vehicles need access.

5 Cars waiting to pick up employees at the end of a shift should park in the road and not in car park.
(You no doubt decided that a reference to Mrs Jarvis's wet shoes was inappropriate!)

Exercise 2

Design and fill in a memo form for the internal message under consideration. Draft a suitable message which includes the five items in the preparatory list. Remember that a combination of tact and firmness is required in order to achieve a 'willing acceptance' by the staff of Mrs Jarvis's decision.

Comment 2

Here is the memo that Sandra drafted and which was found acceptable by Mrs Jarvis.

INTERNAL OFFICE MEMORANDUM

TO   All staff

FROM   A Jarvis

REF   AJ/SK

DATE 3.10.19--

SUBJECT Use of company car park

It will have become obvious to most employees that the car park has become overcrowded recently to the detriment of personal convenience as well as business efficiency.

There have been instances when suppliers' trucks have had severe difficulty in delivering raw materials because of cars temporarily parking in order to pick up employees.

Although it is possible that early next year we will be able to extend the car park, for the time being space is at a premium. It is necessary, therefore, to restrict use of the car park to the following:

(1) Vehicles being the property of Honeypot Biscuits (sales representatives' cars and delivery trucks).

(2) Commercial vehicles delivering supplies for processing.

(3) Vehicles used as personal transport and parked for the duration of an employee's shift.

(4) Visitors to Honeypot Biscuits on commercial business.

It is firmly requested that cars waiting to pick up workers from a shift should park in the road outside. Little personal inconvenience should be caused and the smooth running of our business will be restored.

AJ

Sandy Bay Leisure Services

```
                                          20 Cliffside Drive
                                          SANDY BAY
                                          Dorset
                                          SB7 7TA

                                          5th October 19--


Leisure Services Manager

Dear Sir

     I wish to bring to your attention the casual appearance of many of
your staff.  I have noticed a deterioration in cleanliness and attitude
generally of late.

     I was under the impression that employees of the corporation were
expected to maintain a clean-cut and respectable presence at all times.
During the past month I have been appalled by the greasy hair, dirty
fingernails and sloppy dress displayed by at least half a dozen of the
staff whose jobs for the Leisure Services Dept bring them into contact
with the general public.

     I will not mention the departments concerned as I would not, at
this stage, wish to jeopardize their jobs.  I would suggest, however,
that you have a strong word with your staff as some of them must be
bringing Sandy Bay into disrepute in the eyes of our valuable visitors.

                    Yours faithfully


                    Enid Barry

                    (Enid Barry - Mrs)
```

Tracy read the letter that had recently appeared on her desk once more. Clearly Mr Bickerstaffe had a purpose in leaving it for her attention. She suspected that a letter of apology or enquiry was going to be required of her. Tracy was not sure whether the letter was from a crank or a genuinely insulted member of the public. From her brief experience of the department she thought that it was quite possible that Mrs Barry had a valid cause for complaint.

Mr Bickerstaffe hurried in.

'Tracy, I hope you've had a chance to look through that letter from Mrs Barry. It's made me hopping mad.'

'I have actually, Mr Bickerstaffe. Do you think it's serious?'

'I certainly do. It just confirms an impression I've been getting recently. I meant to do something about it last week but got snowed under with the estimates for next year's entertainments' programme. Some of the department have been getting really scruffy lately. We've got to get this sorted out before we start getting complaints from councillors and the like.'

'Do you want me to write a letter of apology to Mrs Barry?'

'Certainly, but only after you've got a memo sorted out to the offending employees concerned.'

'Who will I send the memos to, Mr Bickerstaffe?'

'That's the problem. Let's think. I suppose the most diplomatic thing would be to send a memo out for the attention of *all* staff in departments that have contact with the general public. Those to whom it doesn't apply won't be offended and, hopefully, those who have got sloppy will recognize the complaint as relevant to themselves.'

'Are you going to dictate the message, Mr Bickerstaffe?'

'No time I'm afraid. I've got a meeting with the Finance Committee in five minutes. Draft a firm memo drawing the staff's attention to the need for cleanliness and neatness of appearance when dealing with the general public in particular. You might mention that the public pays our wages by the rates and use of our facilities. You might also mention that I'll be arranging for random, spot checks at Leisure Department sites in the very near future. I realize that it's only a minority who are being careless about their appearance but everyone could end up with a bad name. I'll see you later to see what you've drafted.'

Assignment

Check the organizational model for Sandy Bay Leisure Services Department in Chapter 6. Decide which sections contain staff who meet the general public and need to receive, therefore, copies of the memo.

Remembering the letter from Mrs Barry and Mr Bickerstaffe's instruction to be firm but diplomatic, draft a suitable memo. You should use standard memorandum layout.

In addition you may wish to write Tracy's later letter of apology to Mrs Barry on Mr Bickerstaffe's behalf. Advice on letters of apology may be found in Chapter 13. A tactful and concise letter is called for which may make brief, general reference to steps being taken by the Leisure Services Department to rectify the cause of complaint.

9 Methods for writing summaries and summarizing correspondence

Writing a summary

Writing a summary involves creating a condensed version of written, or sometimes oral, material, in a logical way that ensures the most important information from the original is included, but in a briefer form. In other words, a summary must include the main points of the original but use fewer words. The original material for the summary may be spoken or written but a written summary of written material is what one is most likely to be requested for in a work situation.

The types of material which often require summary could include: a group discussion, a lecture, a feature article in a newspaper or magazine, a series of letters in correspondence, opinions raised at a meeting.

Selection process

Although it is essential that a summary uses fewer words than the original material, it is equally essential that selection takes place so that the significant or principal points are left and the illustrative or irrelevant discarded. There are two stages to the selection process.

Stage 1 selection

At the first stage we must decide which information needs to be included in the summary and which should be omitted. The material that you leave out is selected for disposal because it is either irrelevant to the main purpose of the summary *or* not likely to need further reference.

Stage 2 selection

Having decided on the material in the original that needs summarizing we move on to classify the material that is left into two categories:

1 That which requires writing about in some detail because of its importance.
2 That which only requires brief reference because of its lesser importance.

The two stages of selection having been completed, it remains to reduce the two categories of material left after the Stage 2 selection into the minimum number of words that will successfuly communicate the essence of the original material. At this stage we are selecting appropriate words rather than material.

Figure 9.1 is a model that may help to simplify the processes described above.

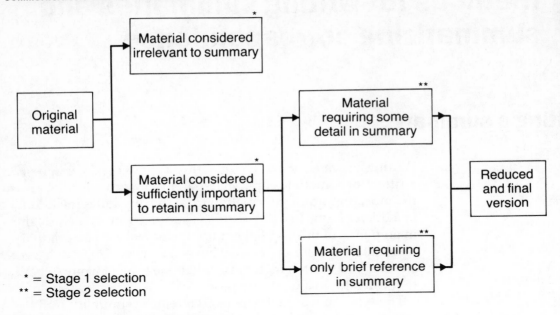

* = Stage 1 selection
** = Stage 2 selection

Figure 9.1 Steps in summary writing

Methods of summarizing

Assuming that the purpose of the summary has been made clear, there are three methods of summarizing written material:

Method 1

With the original words in front of you, the less important words are struck out and the important words which communicate the chief points are retained. If this is done carefully, so as to keep grammatical sense, you are left with reduced material in the writer's own words. The disadvantage of this is that the summary will not be as brief as the other methods.

Method 2

With the writer's original words in front of you, the less important sentences are struck out, leaving complete sentences that contain the chief points. You are left with the most important points, in sentences and in the writer's own words. The disadvantage of this is that not all writers use clear-cut sentences of either significant or insignificant importance. The decision of what to retain and what to reject can be extremely difficult.

Method 3

After reading the original material carefully and making notes of important points, you rewrite the communication in *your own words*. This is traditionally called a précis and it is customary to aim for approximately 30 per cent of the length of the original material in this type of summary.

If we assume that the type of summary most often required on a day-to-day basis is a précis arrived at by Method 3 (above), a system of preparing such a summary could be based on the stages shown in Figure 9.2.

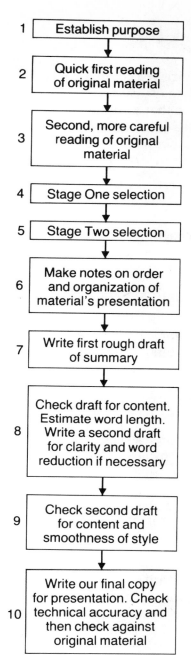

1	Establish purpose
2	Quick first reading of original material
3	Second, more careful reading of original material
4	Stage One selection
5	Stage Two selection
6	Make notes on order and organization of material's presentation
7	Write first rough draft of summary
8	Check draft for content. Estimate word length. Write a second draft for clarity and word reduction if necessary
9	Check second draft for content and smoothness of style
10	Write our final copy for presentation. Check technical accuracy and then check against original material

Figure 9.2   Summary preparation

Figure 9.2 may make the writing of a summary seem rather daunting and something of a prolonged process. It should be said, however, that with practice the process becomes semi-automatic. At first the various stages will take some time, but learning to ride a bike and to drive a car are difficult skills to acquire at first. As in most activities, practice and repetition lead to reasonably easy proficiency eventually. In work as well as in life, skill in summarizing material that is written at length is an important and useful expertise.

The following brief comments on the numbered stages in Figure 9.2 may be of use.

1   Establishing the *purpose* of the summary is usually a matter of ensuring that the instructions given when the summary was requested are clearly understood. Check whether you have been requested to work to a general word limit and whether numbered notes or continuous prose are required.
2   A quick *first reading* of the material is necessary to establish the overall concept and general content of the material to be summarized.
3   A second more *careful reading* of the material allows you to notice (and possibly make notes on) the different sections that contain linked or possibly different material. The paragraphing of the material may help.
4   The *Stage 1* selection process has been dealt with previously.
5   The *Stage 2* selection process has been dealt with previously.
6   *Preparing notes* allows you to begin organizing your version of the original material under subheadings and to decide what needs dealing with in some detail or can be sketched in briefly. You can also decide about the order in which the details are to be presented.
7   The *rough draft* allows you to decide whether your version of the material is in the best order. Although this draft will almost certainly be longer than your final draft, you should be more concerned to check that you have retained only the essential material.
8   Writing a *second draft* after checking the rough draft allows you to reword and restructure sentences in order to get down to the required number of words. You should not need to remove material but concentrate on saying the same things in a more economical way.
9   *Reading* and *checking the second draft* should permit you to concentrate on the style of your writing. It has to be taken for granted that by now you have included the correct material and got down very close to a word limit. You should be checking for accuracy of spelling and punctuation as well as the use of proper sentences.
10   The *final draft* should be accurate, well presented and checked one more time against the original material.

Summarizing correspondence

This kind of summary is required in an office or a company where a series of letters has been received which may deal with different aspects of some common subject. It may be that a number of letters have been received that *complain* of a service provided or a product that is produced. It may, on the other hand, be a number of letters *enquiring* about some particular feature of the company's work.

Three obvious reasons for making summaries of correspondence are:

1 A pattern of correspondence can be recognized which alerts management to a problem or a need that is emerging in the company's activities.
2 The summary of correspondence can be easily circulated through relevant departments so that individuals responsible can quickly check back on individual letters.
3 A summary sheet of correspondence can be filed more economically than a large number of letters, thus saving valuable space.

Layout and organization of material

1 A simple but clear heading is required, eg:

Summary of correspondence between Beckett's Sausages and Trading Standards Officer concerning weights of frozen products (7 July–8 August 19--)
or
Summary of correspondence between Beckett's Sausages and complainants referring to faulty Batch Number 220J (28 June–4 July 19--)

The dates between which the correspondence took place are included in the heading when they are relevant.
2 All informal phrases and emotive language are omitted.
3 Important details that include facts, specifications and matters relevant to the purpose of the correspondence must be retained in the summary.
4 Separate paragraphs are used for each letter referred to in the summary.

Example

Summary of correspondence between Beckett's Sausages and a number of complainants (28 June–4 July 19--)
Agnes Rees of Trafalgar Road, Stroud complained that one of two packets of De-Luxe Beef and Pork Barbecue sausages was underweight when defrosted.

Thomas Atkinson of Beechwood Gardens, Shrewsbury complained that a packet of De-Luxe Beef Fryers purchased from a branch of Greenbank Supermarkets was underweight.

Mary Fletcher of Station Road, Exeter complained that a packet of De-Luxe Beef Fryers was underweight when defrosted and one of the sausages contained a piece of white plastic (2 mm × 8 mm).

Gillian Worth complained that a packet of De-Luxe Beef Fryers was underweight when defrosted and that a piece of white plastic (4 mm × 8 mm) was stuck to the inside of the wrapper.

Each complainant was sent an individual letter of apology which regretted any inconvenience caused and included a £5.00 purchase voucher for any of Beckett's Sausages products.

Assignment

Study each of the following letters of complaint. Assume that you have been given the task of making an organized summary of this correspondence. Bearing in mind the advice for layout which has been given and remembering the example just given, make an appropriate summary of this correspondence.

Charles James
112 Wood Green
BIRMINGHAM
BH7 7AT

2 January 19--

Trusty Canners Ltd
Northern Industrial Estate
NORTHBURY
Wiltshire
N14 5TF

Dear Sir

I feel it my duty to inform you of a most unfortunate experience I have had as a result of purchasing a can of your Petit Pois garden peas last week.

On opening the can I found that there was a fungus growth on the inside of the lid and a most unpleasant taste to the peas themselves. In addition I found that there were traces of rust on the inner seam of the can itself.

I am sure that you would not wish a presumably faulty batch of your product to remain on sale for longer than necessary so thought I should bring this to your attention.

I should like to hear from you with some explanation of this most disturbing lack of quality control.

Yours faithfully

(Charles James)

Audrey Scammel
28 Carter Crescent
WOLVERHAMPTON
WP16 6TL

7 January 19--

Trusty Canners Ltd
Northern Industrial Estate
NORTHBURY
Wiltshire
NY14 5TF

Dear Sir,

I was most impressed by your attempt to bring variety and added protein into my life. You may not be aware that the canned garden peas are now featuring carrots instead of the advertised contents, and include the body of a dead cockroach as an added 'bonus'. Although I managed to consume the carrots and was prepared to forget the cockroach I had to draw the line at the rusty stains that lined the interior of the lid!

I realise that you must be going through troubled times in these difficult economic conditions but I really think you had better get your act together on the hygiene front.

Yours faithfully,

Audrey Scammel
Audrey Scammel

Carole Bleaney
Flat 6
Trafalgar Mansions
Coventry
CV5 11BC

10 January 19--

Trusty Canners Ltd
Northern Industrial Estate
NORTHBURY
Wiltshire
N14 5TF

Dear Sirs

I am reporting the following information regarding the condition of your canned peas direct to the local Trading Standards Office.

On opening a can of your garden peas that I had purchased from Luxel Supermarket in Coventry, I found that the can was distinctly rusty and there was a fungus growth on the top layer of the peas. On emptying the disgusting contents into the waste bin I found a cockroach lying in the bottom of the can.

This type of accident just will not do. A person with poorer eyesight than myself could have eaten the contents with potentially deadly results. I await your comments.

Yours faithfully

Carole Bleaney
(Carole Bleaney)

Comment

You will have noticed that the three letters contained the following references to faults:

1 Rusty can (x3)
2 Stale taste (x1)
3 Wrong label (x1)
4 Fungus growth (x2)
5 Cockroach (x2)

Your summary should certainly contain all the complaints listed above. One letter mentioned involvement of the Trading Standards Office and this should also have been included in your summary.

English in use

Ambiguity resulting from faulty word order

Ambiguity in speech or writing occurs when the sense of a sentence can be taken as having more than one interpretation, eg:

Flying over the valley, the cows appeared contented in the afternoon sun.

In the above example the ambiguity is amusing because the picture that it is possible to visualize if we read the sentence the wrong way is clearly ridiculous. The communication process breaks down as we are distracted from the true intention of the sentence by the silly mental image of flying cows.

It is important in the world of work that our writing of letters, memos, notices, etc, does not include sentences that can be interpreted in more than one way. Misunderstandings, confusion and ill-feeling can easily result when one group of readers makes one interpretation and another group makes a different interpretation.

The most common cause of ambiguity in sentences is *faulty word order*. There are other causes of ambiguity which will be dealt with briefly at the end of the chapter. The problem of sentences containing words or phrases in *the wrong proximity* to each other is the chief cause of misinterpretation, eg:

We only believe in female ministers preaching in church.

In this case the placing of the word 'only' leads to three possible interpretations:

1 We are the sole people to believe in female ministers being allowed to preach in church.
2 We believe that the only people who should be allowed to preach in church are female ministers.
3 When we hear preaching we believe solely in what female ministers preach (possibly disbelieving male ministers).

This is because 'only' in the original example can apply to both 'we' and 'believe'. If we move 'only' to a place in the sentence where it can apply to either 'we' or 'believe' (but *not* to both) then we end up with either:

1 *Only* we believe in female ministers preaching in church.
or
2 We believe *only* in female ministers preaching in church.

The general rule to remember is that words or phrases which qualify other words or phrases must be placed in close proximity to avoid possible ambiguity.

Other causes of ambiguity

1   *Sentences that omit necessary words*
For example:
   The umpire said the batsman was drunk.
If we wish to make it clear who is drunk on the field of play we must use 'that' to clear up the ambiguity, eg:
   The umpire said *that* the batsman was drunk.
2   *Sentences that use words of double meaning*
   For example:
      She grumbled since she missed the train.
   The word 'since' can refer to either the time when the grumbling commenced or the cause of the grumbling.
3   *Sentences that confuse because of careless use of pronouns*
   For example:
      Anna told Helen that *she* would be going for training next month.
   As the above example is written it is impossible to decide which of the two nouns (Anna or Helen) the pronoun 'she' stands for. We do not know, therefore, who is going for training.

10 Ongoing case studies

Honeypot Biscuits

Sandra looked through the morning's letters that lay in Mrs Jarvis's 'in-tray'. She had asked her to check through her morning's mail as a conference of northern confectionery manufacturers required her presence most of the day. When she returned, sometime in the afternoon, she needed to have a quick glance at the main topics of correspondence that had arrived in her absence.

Fortunately for Sandra, who had to make a summary of correspondence for Mrs Jarvis, there was not a great quantity of letters on this particular morning.

Here are the letters that were addressed to Mrs Jarvis by name:

NORTHERN MILLERS Ltd.

Grange Industrial Estate

Upper Grangeforth

Cumbria GF11 9AB

18 October 19--

A Jarvis
Managing Director
Honeypot Biscuits
Haworth Lane
MILHAM
Lancashire
BB12 9PN

Dear Mrs Jarvis

We have been experiencing some difficulties with supplies of hard wheat grain from our traditional suppliers. Alternative supplies of a grain that would allow us to produce a medium-hard flour at competitive rates have been arranged.

As you are a valued customer of our products, and as we pride ourselves on offering a tailor-made service to our clients, we would like to send one of our technical representatives to visit your plant.

Would it be convenient if our representative came to discuss our new range of flours with you towards the end of next week? He would bring samples and specifications as well as a cost analysis of new baking methods that may be required.

Yours sincerely

Charles Fleer

(Charles Fleer - Customer Services)

49

FACTORY INSPECTORATE

Branch NR2
24 Brook Gate
YORK
YB17 4FD

18 October 19--

A Jarvis
Managing Director
Honeypot Biscuits
Haworth Lane
MILHAM
Lancashire BB12 9PN

Dear Mrs Jarvis

We wish to inform you that your plant and machinery will be subject to an inspection on 24 October next week.

Mrs Anderson, who is responsible for the North-West region, will arrive at 8.00 am and we would appreciate it if you would render whatever assistance she requires relating to access and information.

Her inspection will last approximately four hours after which she will give you an informal report of her findings prior to a written report which will follow at a later date.

Please confirm receipt of this notice at your earliest convenience.

Yours sincerely

Alan Crabtree

(Alan Crabtree - Chief Inspector)

K

Managing Director
Honeypot Biscuits
Haworth Lane
MILHAM
Lancs BB12 9PN

Ken's Korner Konfectionery

12 Hall Street
MILHAM
Lancs MH3 7JY

17 October 19--

Dear Mrs Jarvis

I'm afraid I must complain about the state of a batch of Oat Crunch Fingers which were delivered yesterday. I was not in the shop when the delivery was made but when unpacking the boxes a few hours later found that a two dozen container box of Oat Crunch Fingers contained a large number of crushed and broken packets.

The container box showed signs of crushing and I can only assume that the damage occurred in transit from your works.

If you would inform your driver of this incident I will leave the damaged Oat Crunch Fingers for his inspection when he delivers next week. I assume a credit note will be issued. I thought you would wish to be informed of this incident in case similar accidents have been reported from other retailers.

Yours sincerely
Kenneth Sagar

(Kenneth Sagar - Proprietor)

The Manager
Honeypot Biscuits
Haworth Lane
MILHAM
Lancs BB12 9PN

25 Larch Street
MILHAM
Lancs
17th October 19--

Dear Madam

I am writing to enquire whether I could be considered for a job at Honeypot Biscuits. I left school last year and have worked at a variety of part time posts since that time.

I am taking my motorcycle test next month and thought I might be useful to you as a courier. I have three G.C.S.E. passes and a bronze medal in life saving.

I look forward to hearing from you.

Yours faithfully

Craig Sumner

MILHAM COLLEGE OF FURTHER EDUCATION
-------------- DEPARTMENT OF BUSINESS STUDIES --------------
Leeds Road : Milham : Lancashire : BB8 6YT

18 October 19--

A Jarvis
Managing Director
Honeypot Biscuits
Haworth Lane
MILHAM
Lancashire BB12 9PN

Dear Mrs Jarvis

As a tutor on the CPVE course run at our college I am responsible for arranging a programme of guest speakers whose expertise is relevant to the business element in the course.

Since you are a business woman with a developing company, it would be most useful for our students to hear from you and have the opportunity to ask questions.

If you would consent to address a group of students for about half an hour on the general topic of 'risk taking' in the small business and answer questions afterwards I would be most grateful.

If you would inform me whether you would consent to give us a talk and what dates and times would be convenient to you, I will make arrangements at this end.

Yours sincerely

Jean Watson.

(Jean Watson - Course Tutor)

Milham Health Stores
The Precinct
MILHAM
Lancashire BB4 9PK   . ... *for all your Health Needs*

17 October 19--

The Manager
Honeypot Biscuits
Haworth Lane
MILHAM
Lancashire
BB12 9PN

Dear Madam

    I wish to complain most strongly about the condition of some stock
ordered from your company last week. When the order was delivered on
16 October I found the following:

(1) Eight packets of Sesame Cookies had damaged outer wrappers.

(2) A dozen packets of Oat Crunch Fingers were crushed.

    Since our business depends upon the high quality of our goods, I am
most disappointed in the state of these items. Your delivery driver
suggested that I get in touch with you if I had cause for complaint.

    I must say that I consider his attitude most reprehensible and wish
to register the strongest possible dissatisfaction.

    I trust that you will take steps to replace the damaged goods at
the earliest possible opportunity.

            Yours faithfully

            Margot Hughes

            (Margot Hughes - Proprietor)

Milham Ladies Club
c/o Claire Rimmer
20 Moor Court
MILHAM
Lancashire
BB9 8QT

18 October 19--

The Managing Director
Honeypot Biscuits
Haworth Lane
MILHAM
Lancashire
BB12 9PN

Dear Mrs Jarvis

    I am sure you will be aware of the activites of the Milham Ladies
Club. Our guest speakers and trips out are extremely popular with the
membership.

    As this year's secretary I am busy designing the programme of
activities for the second half of the year. I would like to arrange for
a guided tour of your factory if this was agreeable with you.

    There would be approximately fifteen visitors and we normally try
to occupy about an hour and a half on our visits out. If you feel that
you could permit such a visit, preferably some convenient weekday
afternoon in June, perhaps you would be so kind as to contact me.

    I trust that this request does not intrude too much on your
valuable time.

            Yours sincerely

            Claire Rimmer

            (Claire Rimmer - Secretary)

Assignment

Draft a summary of correspondence for Mrs Jarvis. You should take note of the layout and suggestions made in the previous chapter. Two of the letters contain information that could be damaging to Honeypot Biscuits' reputation and trading. Ensure that the information in these two, separate, letters is presented in such a way that Mrs Jarvis's attention is drawn to a possible pattern.

Sandy Bay Leisure Services

Mr Bickerstaffe has phoned to say that he is sick. He has said that he will be back at work tomorrow. His instructions to Tracy are to go through his mail and make a summary of the *essential correspondence* with which he will have to deal immediately he returns to the office.

Tracy has already put a dozen letters aside that are general enquiries and which she can either deal with herself or bring to Mr Bickerstaffe's attention at a later date. She is left with the following letters. She is uncertain whether they are all *essential* correspondence.

Seacrest Garden Centre
Meadow Crescent
SANDY BAY
Dorset SB117 6BB

Sandy Bay Leisure Services
The Promenade
SANDY BAY
Dorset
SB15 7CB

20 October 19--

Dear Sir

We are clearing our greenhouses for the arrival of new stock. There are a number of house plants that have grown too large for domestic purchase.

I should like to present them for possible decoration of the Municipal Hall or some other venue. There would, naturally, be no charge.

All we would ask is that you provide transport to take them away. We are in desperate need for the space they are occupying and if I do not hear from you by Monday of next week at the latest I shall have to dispose of them by some alternative means.

Yours faithfully

(Peter Hesketh - Proprietor)

The Director
Sandy Bay Leisure Services
The Promenade
SANDY BAY
Dorset
SB 15 7CB

12 Reed Street
SANDY BAY
Dorset
SB 11 4UY

19 October 19--

Dear Sir

While attending a concert held by the Sandy Bay Orpheus Choir at the Library Arts Centre last week, I was most disgusted by the low level of heating in the auditorium.

My enjoyment of the splendid performance of English Sea Shanties was completely ruined by the miserably cold conditions the audience was apparently expected to endure.

On due consideration I have decided that I want my money back or else I shall be forced to take this matter up with a higher authority.

Yours faithfully

Jean Alexander

(Jean Alexander- Rate Payer)

SLADE CENTRAL TALENT
6-8 Palmeira Gardens
Hampstead
LONDON NW99 8WW . . . .
19 October 19--

The Director
Sandy Bay Leisure Services
The Promenade
SANDY BAY
Dorset
SB15 7CB

Dear Mr Bickerstaffe

I shall be in Sandy Bay on Friday 22 October for the day. I should like to call in to talk with you about a touring group I represent. 'The Magic Mystery Theatre' have appeared in a number of resorts on the south coast and play to an average of 85 per cent capacity audiences.

I could offer you a booking at an especially attractive rate as they already have a booking in Bournemouth which is quite close to you. Since their travel expenses will already be looked after the rate would be about £75.00 less than they normally charge.

Please contact me on 01-738-33661 if you would be interested in discussing possible hire of this family entertainment group.

Yours sincerely

(Maurice Slade - Director)

SANDY BAY DRAMATIC SOCIETY

c/o Miles Newman
68 Latimer Avenue
SANDY BAY
Dorset
SB10 4ER

19 October 19--

G Bickerstaffe
Director
Sandy Bay Leisure Services
The Promenade
SANDY BAY
Dorset
SB15 7CB

Dear Mr Bickerstaffe

The Sandy Bay Dramatic Society, of which I am the secretary, is seeking a venue for its annual festival of one act plays. We have previously rented the Hippodrome Theatre from its private owners but their rental charges this year have increased beyond our means.

The committee is considering holding the festival in a neighbouring town which can offer a venue we can afford. I am reluctant to take this step and would first like to enquire the rates you could offer for a three night rental of the Library Arts Centre in the last week of November.

I have to present a response to the committee which meets on Sunday. My apologies for the short notice of this enquiry but events have developed quickly.

Yours sincerely

(Miles Newman - Secretary)

---

40 Wellington Road
CHESTER
CT10 4BZ

18 October 19--

The Director
Sandy Bay Leisure Services
SANDY BAY
Dorset SB15 7CB

Dear Sir

I am engaged in writing a book, which has been commissioned by Heathcote Publishing, on the history of British seaside resorts. I have been advised that I should feature only three Dorset resorts.

My original plan was to include six resorts in Dorset, including Sandy Bay. I would still like to include Sandy Bay but my decision must now be based on the access that I might be given to archive material and historical photographs of the area.

I must make my decision within the week and would, therefore, be grateful if you could inform me of what cooperation I might receive in researching your resort.

Yours faithfully

(Charlotte Rayner)

Assignment

Decide whether all five letters need to be summarized. If you believe there are any that do not require Mr Bickerstaffe's *immediate* attention put them aside. Using standard layout, incorporate the *important* information of the priority letters into a *summary of essential correspondence.*

11 Synthesizing of information

The above heading has nothing to do with music although the process of synthesizing is what that aid to modern musicians – the synthesizer – does with the aid of microchips and memory. In the world of work you are your own synthesizer and with the aid of your brain and some imagination you perform the function of *'making a whole out of parts'*. (A good dictionary will also define the process of synthesizing as *'the combining of separate elements into a whole'*.)

Synthesizing is what we do almost from the moment when, as toddlers, we learn to speak. Whenever we seek information from a source and put into some sort of pattern we are making a synthesis. For example, asking for information from parents, teachers and classmates is the basis of much knowledge.

Let us imagine a youngster going through a typical process of synthesizing information.

1   *To friend*
    – Do you have a two wheeler bicycle?
    – Did you get it for your birthday?
    – What kind is it?
    – Is it a good runner?

2   *To shopkeeper*
    – Is that a Duplex cycle in the window?
    – How much does it cost?

3   *To mother*
    – How much did you think you might spend on my birthday present?

4   *To father*
    – Can I have a Duplex bicycle from City Cycles for my birthday? It costs £65.00 and Tony who lives down the road has already got one.

In the above simplified example, the process of synthesizing took place using Tony, shopkeeper and mother. The synthesis had been made by the time the father was told the final piece of information.

Other sources the youngster could have used to arrive at a synthesis are: other retailers, other friends, advertising literature, catalogues, trade magazines and consumer reports. The person needing to make a synthesis of information will seek for facts and opinions wherever information is stored and available. Obvious general sources of information are given below.

People

The example of the youngster seeking a bicycle for his birthday was a simple demonstration of the way information and opinion are often to be found, sometimes at a fairly basic level, from people close to hand.

In our youth we tend to use *parents, teachers and peers* as a source of information when we are trying to create a synthesis. The information that a young person would receive from the three groups mentioned above when asking, 'Where do babies come from?' would vary in quality and accuracy but ultimately the enquirer would arrive at a (hopefully) accurate synthesis.

There is a limit to the usefulness of people as sources of information. People's knowledge and experience vary and even if the people concerned do have the information that is required they are going to become irritated if you intrude too often on their time when another source might easily be available. Elsewhere in this book the reader is reminded that when writing letters requesting information one should always realize that the recipient of the letter is doing the enquirer a favour. When asking a person for information face to face it is essential to adopt an appropriate tone of voice and to thank him or her for his or her efforts. It is also advisable to check that the information sought is not available from an easily accessible alternative source.

Encyclopaedias

These are usually available in libraries and can vary from expensive sets with many volumes published by Britannica to single volume encyclopaedias offered by Pears.

An encyclopaedia attempts to cover all knowledge in a general fashion and is set out alphabetically. Since it would be impossible to detail all that there is to know on a subject in any encyclopaedia and since encyclopaedias date very rapidly in some areas of their contents, it is wise to use such a source sparingly and only for background information of a basic nature.

Reference works

These may be found, sometimes, in an office where a particular need for a certain type of information frequently exists. A stamp dealer will, no doubt, have a fairly up-to-date edition of *Stanley Gibbons Stamp Catalogue* on the premises. The reference work is normally a book that is not intended for reading from cover to cover but is useful for checking specific details of required information.

In Chapter 19 assistance is given on use of a library and a book index system. With a little experience it becomes reasonably easy to *find the reference book* required and then, using the book index, *find the appropriate section* of the reference work with the desired information.

Dictionaries

A large number of people keep a dictionary by their side because they believe themselves to be poor spellers. This may be the case, although in order to look up a word you must be able to spell it with a fair degree of accuracy or you wouldn't be able to find it!

A dictionary contains a lot more information than the spelling and meaning of words. The various meanings of a word defined in the dictionary allow us to select the most precise word to communicate our meaning when writing. We can discover how a word is pronounced, what its origin is and whether it is a noun or adjective or verb, etc.

It is necessary to learn how to use a dictionary as there are often abbreviations used in order to condense the large amount of information contained into a reasonable size. You should familiarize yourself with your dictionary so that it can be used quickly as well as efficiently.

Filing system

In the world of work the everyday information you might require is often to be found in a central or departmental filing system. With developments in various methods of electronic information storage this can be a very specialized area. Courses of training are given by companies that use such items as data banks or microfiche information retrieval modules. Cost and relative ease of operation mean that, for a small business, the filing cabinet or box files are still where most information and records are stored.

There are many methods that can be adopted for filing information. The simplest (but crudest) system would be to use a simple alphabetical system. This would probably create more problems than it solved, however. If a person named Brown wrote a letter complaining of the lateness of trains on his local branch line, how would British Rail file the letter if it was operating a simple alphabetical system?

Would it be filed under *B* for Brown?
Would it be filed under *C* for complaint?
Would it be filed under *L* for lateness?
Would it be filed under *T* for trains?

From this ludicrous example, it is quite clear that a more logical and sophisticated system is required, even in a small office or business.

Whether one is filing or searching for information in box files, filing cabinets or electronic retrieval systems (see Chapter 37), a key index is necessary so that the user can recognize the system being used. It should also be noted that finding the information is only half of the problem when using a system. If chaos and ill-feeling from one's fellow workers is to be avoided, it is essential that the information is replaced in the system in the correct place. Once you realize that others depend upon the system as well as yourself, the greater care is likely to be taken over input and extraction when using files.

The purpose of filing, whether it is done physically or electronically, is to enable documents or other information to be found quickly when needed.

Information on electronic sorting and file handling will be found in Chapter 37.

What is filed?

Much of the material to be filed will consist of letters that have been received by the business. Replies to letters will also have to be filed. Details of orders, equipment, finances, etc, must also be kept on file for the smooth running of the business.

Where does material get filed?

When deciding at what point in the filing system to store an item, especially a letter, the method used must always remain the same. The point in the file where a document is placed and from which it is retrieved is the filing point.

How is the filing point decided?

If a letter is to be filed then the filing point can be a date, initial or number. If the item received is a business letter with a printed letter head containing the name of the firm, followed by the address, telephone and possibly telex number, then the filing point is the name of the firm. A letter in reply will also be filed at the same point.

If a letter is received which is a personal business letter, without a firm's name and address, then the filing point will be the name of the sender of the letter (ie the signature at the bottom). Replies to such letters will have the same filing point as the name of the original sender. These documents will be filed alphabetically.

What is numerical filing?

Since a business will be involved with filing invoices, receipts, quotations, orders, etc, there is a need for such frequently received items to be filed numerically.

The filing point for such items will usually be the particular number on the invoice, order, etc. These documents will be filed in ascending order of number.

What is cross-referencing?

When a company with which business is done changes its name, due to a takeover, merger or some other reason, it will take some time for this to become known by all who use the file system. A file is opened under a new filing point with the new name and documents refiled. The old name will be retained in the system for some time but instead of documents, a cross-referencing sheet will be filed. On this the new name and other major details will be found in order to refer the user of the file to the new filing point.

You will be familiar with having to do the same sort of thing when a friend gets married and changes her surname. It will be necessary to change her position in your address book or personal telephone pad. You may, for a time, still look her up under her old name but will have made a note by the old entry to refer yourself to her new name and address.

Similarly, where details of goods or products on file could be stored under a number of headings, cross-referencing is necessary to avoid duplication or confusion, eg: details of suppliers of staplers, drawing pins, paper clips would be filed under Office Equipment and cross-reference sheets indicating this placed appropriately in the file.

What happens when a file is borrowed?

It is essential for efficiency that a filing clerk will not allow paper or files to be taken away from the storage system without a record being kept. After all, a library will not let you borrow a book without a record being kept of the withdrawal and return, so why should a file be treated less seriously?

All that is needed is a card or sheet that can be placed in the file at the appropriate point when the contents are borrowed. This 'borrower sheet' will usually record:

1   The name or number of the file.
2   The borrower's name.
3   The office or department of the borrower.
4   The date the file was borrowed.
5   The date the file was returned.
6   The signature of the borrower.

Some of the details given above will suggest the responsibilities and duties of a *filing clerk*.

(a)   Acting on instructions from a 'superior' to open or close files as required.
(b)   Collecting and sorting papers to be filed.
(c)   Checking on filing points for items received.
(d)   Filing copies of letters of reply in appropriate filing point.
(e)   Checking and completing cross-referencing sheets.
(f)   Keeping the files well organized and up to date.
(g)   Lending files to company employees after ensuring that a record has been made of the file or material borrowed and the name of the borrower.

Directories

A directory with which everyone is familiar is a telephone directory. Provided that you know the spelling of a person's surname and his or her forename initial, it is possible to find the address and telephone number with reasonable speed.

The 'Yellow Pages', which is a more specialized telephone directory, gives details of local business and organizations that are often of great value for reference.

The standard telephone directory is organized alphabetically by individual's surnames whereas a 'Yellow Pages' directory is classified according to the business or profession of the subscribers. Entries at the beginning of this kind of directory will include Abattoirs, Accountants and Agricultural Contractors, for example. The last few pages will include Vending Machine Service, Washing Machine Retailers and Zinc Products Dealers.

Many specialist businesses or professions will have their own directories (some of which will be in the reference section of a local library), eg Directory of Colleges of Further Education or a Manufacturers and Merchants' Directory. Directories of various kinds are useful in business for the following purposes:

1   Checking names and addresses of individuals and businesses.
2   Finding details of other manufacturers or service companies.
3   Arranging a mailing list for an advertising campaign.
4   Arranging for quotations or estimates from a number of companies in a particular trade or profession.

It might surprise you to visit the reference section of your town or college library and discover the range of information available in a small number of directories. See whether you can find details of shuttlecock manufacturers, Anglican bishops, magazines and newspapers, annual music festivals, arts associations, general practitioners, cricketers. You may find the following directories useful: *Wisden, Willings Press Guide, Crockfords, The Medical Directory, British Music Year Book, Kompass, Directory of British Associations*.

Trade catalogues

A trade catalogue is more than simply a price list. With prices changing so rapidly a catalogue would soon be out of date and require expensive revision and reprinting if prices and catalogues were not kept separate. A price list is what it says whereas a catalogue is usually a list with descriptions and specifications of items (or sometimes services) that are for sale. The catalogue will often be illustrated with line drawings or photographs to enable a potential customer to arrive at a decision whether or not to purchase.

The trade catalogue allows:

1 A firm to bring its product or services to the attention of the public.
2 Enquiries from customers to be checked and answered by reference to the catalogue.
3 A company to check on products that it might need to purchase to maintain its own operation.
4 A company to check on a rival's products or services.

Teletext

BBC and ITV broadcasting stations in Britain operate an information service which is constantly updated hour by hour. For a reasonably small fee the television monitor can be adjusted to allow information that is centrally stored at the headquarters to be displayed on the screen and different 'pages' selected at the press of a remote control button.

Some businesses find the constantly updated information on such things as news, share prices, weather, road traffic conditions, ferry delays, etc, very useful to their business operations. The most popular teletext services offered at the moment are Oracle, Ceefax, 4Tel and Prestel.

Libraries

These are dealt with specifically in Chapter 19 but brief mention should be made of the extra facilities that exist in a library in addition to books. Most reasonable size libraries today will provide access to information via such developments as film strips, audio and sometimes video cassettes, topic files as well as stored back issues of newspapers, magazines and journals. (Sometimes back numbers are on microfilm.)

Miscellaneous

Some sources of information do not fit easily into categories. Such items as timetables, maps, A to Z street guides, atlases and consumer reports may be purchased or found in libraries. They may be used frequently or infrequently depending upon the nature of the business and one's job within the system. Each item mentioned in this miscellaneous category is likely to be of some use at some time.

Assignment

Assume you have been given the task of arranging for a full-day visit to your group by an executive from the London headquarters of some large, national organization. We could take the Director General of the BBC as an example.

You are required to:

1   Find his full business address and phone number.
2   Find the times of suitable trains or possibly air shuttle services from London to your nearest station or airport. (He will need to arrive late morning and will be staying overnight and leaving early the next morning for London.)
3   Arrange and cost suitable hotel accommodation in your town.
4   Arrange and cost a taxi from station/airport to hotel.
5   Familiarize yourself with the biography and career background of your visitor.

You should:

(a)   Decide what sources of information you will need to exploit in order to satisfy the above requirements.
(b)   Familiarize yourself with handling these sources by actually making a synthesis of information in response to the five requirements above.

12 Ongoing case studies

Honeypot Biscuits

Mrs Jarvis had decided it was time to improve the quality of the lighting in the production area of Honeypot Biscuits. Since the demand for the company's products was running so high an evening shift had been in operation for several months. Although the lighting was just adequate, Mrs Jarvis was considering changing over to a more efficient and possibly more economic system.

'I think we'll have all the bulb lighting in Number One and Number Two production bays replaced by fluorescent tubes, Sandra. I need to have quite a bit of information before I go ahead.'

It was Sandra's task to find the required information and put it together into a form which would allow Mrs Jarvis to reach a quick but informed decision.

The information she required was:

1 How is the lighting strength of a fluorescent tube measured and how many tubes would be required to replace 20 light bulbs of 150 watt capacity?
2 What is the price range of fluorescent tubes and the required fitments available from wholesale merchants in the area?
3 What local electrical contractors would be available to do the required contract work and what quotations would they offer for the work necessary?
4 What are the average running costs of a tube light compared to an equivalent bulb or number of bulbs?
5 What is the average life of a tube light compared to a bulb?

Assignment

This is a particularly practical assignment and after reminding yourself of general sources of information available, which were outlined in Chapter 11, you should attempt to find the answers to the five enquiry areas that Mrs Jarvis instructed Sandra to investigate. You should use your own local area as the setting for your enquiries. A college or town library would be a good starting point.

1 List the sources used with the general headings given in the previous chapter as well as the particular examples actually approached, eg Directory – Thomson Local Directory and Yellow Pages. The above would be only one part of your list.
2 By actually trying to find answers to Mrs Jarvis's enquiries, supply brief noted answers or estimates to the five questions.

Sandy Bay Leisure Services

Mr Bickerstaffe had received the following letter from an organization of senior citizens who had booked the Municipal Hall for a one-day convention in three weeks' time.

AGE ALLEGIANCE

14 PELMAN GARDENS - LONDON - NW9 6DB

The Director   26 October 19--
Sandy Bay Leisure Services
Town Hall
The Promenade
Sandy Bay

Dear Sir

        I am writing to confirm our booking of the Sandy Bay Municipal Hall
on Wednesday 19 November. I am sure that, as in previous years, this
useful and enjoyable event will run smoothly and efficiently.

        As we agreed on first booking, the hall will be required to be laid
out with seating for 600 while the addresses from the platform take
place in the morning and afternoon. I understand from our phone call of
17 August that you have managed to book the Henry Hathaway Memorial Band
for the dancing in the evening.

        It has been pointed out to me by the coordinating committee that
many of the delegates at the conference will be of advanced years and
might welcome the opportunity for a rest and some entertainment during
an interval in the dancing. I wonder if it would be possible for you to
contact and book a suitable act to provide entertainment for about 30 to
40 minutes in the middle of the evening? I have been told that we could
afford a fee of approximately £150 for such an entertainer.

        I am sorry to put you to this trouble at comparatively short notice
but we would be most obliged if you could let me know of any acts that
might be available so that we can confirm a booking by return of post.

        Yours faithfully

        Eric Chamberley

        (Eric Chamberley - Secretary)

Tracy was given the task of finding the *availability, suitability* and *fee* of an act to entertain during the interval in dancing at the Age Allegiance convention.

The sources of information she used were as follows:

1   *People*   Tracy contacted people she knew in the Social Services Department of Sandy Bay who had organized entertainments and outings for senior citizens in the district. The general opinion was that older people had little patience with magic acts or ventriloquists, although impressionists and music hall style singers were much appreciated.

2   *Filing system*   Checking back through the office files Tracy found the details of local entertainers who had performed at functions in the town in the past. There seemed to be a large number of magicians and ventriloquists. She did, however, manage to find the names, addresses and telephone numbers of some theatrical agents from the files.

3   *Library*   In the reading room of the Sandy Bay library Tracy found the current edition of *The Stage*. In the classified adverts at the back of this journal she found a large number of entertainers advertising their availability as well as more details of theatrical agents.

4   *Directories*   Using the telephone directory Tracy found the telephone numbers of four possibly suitable acts and phoned these to check on availability and normally required fee.

Having made some notes, Tracy made a synthesis of the information she had gathered and put it in the form of a memo to Mr Bickerstaffe.

INTERNAL OFFICE MEMORANDUM

REF ....TD/EC

DATE .29..10.19--

TO   ...Mr..A..Bickerstaffe
FROM .....Tracy..Donaldson

SUBJECT.........ENTERTAINER..SUITABLE..FOR..AGE..ALLEGIANCE CONVENTION

The following entertainers, who have been contacted by telephone, are available to provide a 45 minute entertainment spot at the Municipal Hall on Wednesday 19 November.

(1)   Charles 'The voice of them all' Strange. He has performed for senior citizens' groups in the past and his agent claims he is very popular with the older generation. His fee would be £85.00.

(2)   Carole Keen, comedy impressionist. Two of our staff have seen her in performance in pier shows on the east coast. They say she is quite popular with male members of an audience but is not so much appreciated by females. Her fee would be £105.00.

(3)   'Wandering Willy - The Singing Kilt'. This is a relatively new entertainer whose act consists of comic impressions of turn-of-the-century Scottish music hall artists. A review of his act in a theatrical journal praised him, although some of his material can verge on the obscene at times. His fee is £65.00 plus expenses.

(4)   Laura Lynne - The Irish Thrush. An established entertainer whose act is a light hearted impression of a number of Victorian music hall singers. Her agent says she is particularly skilled at getting community singing going in an audience. She has worked on cruise ships specializing in holidays for the elderly. Her fee is £125.00 plus expenses.

TD

13 Letters of apology, complaint and requesting information

Letters of apology are usually written in response to letters of complaint. The latter will be dealt with in the following case studies. First, we will look at the response that is required when handling a letter of complaint.

Letter of apology

There is a variety of reasons for writing a letter of apology in the world of business and, therefore, a number of styles:

1 The company may be in the wrong and wish to keep the business and approval of a customer while offering compensation in some form.
2 The company may not accept total responsibility for the complaint and wish to offer its regrets and placate the customer while avoiding any financial or other commitment.
3 The company may feel itself totally free of guilt in the situation but wish to offer some form of recompense for the customer's inconvenience in order to keep goodwill and further business.

Examples Here are examples of each type in the same order as above.

1

Avion Skylink

100 Chelmsley Way
Ridgehampton
Surrey
ST9 9KL

12 August 19--

Margaret Akabuwe
7 Dupont Avenue
DORKING
Surrey
DK16 9PK

Dear Mrs Akabuwe

    We are extremely sorry to learn of the damage to your suitcase while travelling on our minibus from Dorking centre to Gatwick. We have spoken to the driver concerned and he confirms that he had not stacked the case in the luggage compartment according to our normal procedure.

    We hope that your holiday was not spoiled to any large degree and would like to offer you the enclosed cheque for £18.00 to compensate you for replacement of the article concerned and any inconvenience to yourself.

    I do hope that we can look forward to arranging any other holiday that you take in the future.

Yours sincerely

Alison Whittle

(Alison Whittle - Customer Services)

2

BADGER CRISPS Ltd

17 Huncoat Way Clutterbridge Estate Clutterbridge Derbyshire CL12 8HJ

6 May 19--

Clive Doidge
25 Spenser Ave
SPENTHAM
Yorkshire
SP11 2GZ

Dear Mr Doidge

We were extremely sorry to hear of your disappointment with a
packet of our Barbecued Prawn crisps. We have examined the empty packet
that you kindly sent with your letter of complaint. It is clear from
the manufacturing code on the packet that the 'sell by' date had been
overlooked by the retailer from whom you purchased the packet.

We have contacted Supervalue Supermarkets and asked them to check
their shelf stock. We realize that this is no compensation to your self
and hope that you will accept the enclosed purchase certificate which is
exchangeable for any of our products to the value of £5.00.

We hope that this unfortunate incident will not affect your
appreciation of our products and that you will continue to be a valued
customer.

Yours sincerely

Deirdre Ashburn

(Deirdre Ashburn - Consumer Relations)

3

Scrummy Beans Ltd
Ditchfield Road
Ditchfield
Hertfordshire
DT18 5ER

24 July 19--

A K Patel
14 Hart Street
KILBARN
Fifeshire
KB6 6YT

Dear Mr Patel

We were most disturbed to hear of the trouble you have experienced
with one of our products. From your letter it appears that you have
misread the instructions on the label. Our Scrummy Butter Beans are not
intended to be served on toast as they are not in any form of sauce.
They are intended to be used in salads or as part of a recipe. I can
assure you that our Scrummy Baked Beans are excellent when served as a
snack.

I have pleasure in enclosing one of our recipe leaflets and hope
that in future you will find many uses for our products.

Yours sincerely

Arthur Woburn

(Arthur Woburn - Customer Services)

You will have recognized that although the three letters are accepting varying degrees of responsibility, each adopts a courteous and friendly tone. The balance of tone is important. Letter 1, which accepts full responsibility, does not descend to a grovelling level while at the other end, letter 3, which is denying responsibility, does not adopt an abusive tone when pointing out the customer's stupidity.

Whatever the degree of responsibility being accepted by the company it is important that a concerned and caring tone is used in the letter of apology. It is not a case of the customer always being right; it is a matter of a customer who has been annoyed sufficiently to write a letter of complaint needing to be calmed down and put in a mood that will ensure his or her continued custom.

Each letter expresses concern at the customer's unhappiness and goes on to offer some form of explanation and concludes with the hope that future custom will continue to be placed. Imagine yourself as the recipient of these letters of apology and try to estimate your feelings on receiving each. How would you feel? Would you continue to use the company's products or services? Would you feel satisfied? Whenever you have reason to write a letter of apology always imagine yourself as the complainant and judge its suitability by your own needs as an aggrieved customer.

Assignment

Here are three letters of complaint. Reply to each in the manner you believe to be appropriate and offering the compensation you believe justifiable.

1

Hurst Stores
High Street
Skipton
West Yorkshire

Freda Chadwick
11 Helmshore Road
Giggleswick
West Yorkshire
18 November 19--

Dear Sirs

Having purchased a Rodin Studios figurine of 'The Little Shepherd Girl' from your store on Saturday I was most disappointed to unwrap my purchase at home and discover that 'The Little Shepherd Girl' had become 'St George Slaying the Dragon'.

As the purchase was intended for my niece's birthday next week I am most angry at this stupid mistake. I would like to know what you intend to do about this ridiculous mix up.

Yours faithfully
Freda Chadwick

(Miss Freda Chadwick)

2

Jolly Toys Ltd
Gresham Industrial Estate
GRESHAM
Lincolnshire
GH 12 7 TK

George Calthrop
77 The Causeway
BRICKFIELD
Staffordshire
BK 12 2BW
23 August 19--

Dear Sir
   I recently received a gift for my birthday of a Whirly Wing helicopter gun ship, manufactured by your company. I assembled it according to the instructions only to find that it did not work.
   My friend who has a similar model told me that it needs batteries to work but none were provided with the packing. Please send me some batteries right away.
                              Yours faithfully

                              George Calthrop

                              (George Calthrop)

Juicy Jellies

Wisbech Road
Wisbech
Cambridgeshire
WB11 9PH

Wisbech Fruit Estates
Longbarrow Road
WISBECH
Cambridgeshire
WB12 3QP

6 March 19--

Dear Sirs

   I should like to inform you that your last delivery of strawberries and strawberry pulp was sub-standard with regard to weight and colour. The weight discrepancy was only three pounds per ton but the colour was disappointingly insipid.

   Although we could use artificial colouring to remedy the colour loss we are loath to do so as our trading agreement is quite specific regarding colour and quality of product purchased from your estates.

   We do not wish to involve the Trading Standards Office at this stage since there have been many happy years of cooperation between our two companies but we must have a satisfactory response from you on this important matter.

        Yours faithfully

        Mansoor Hussein

        (Mansoor Husein - Quality Control)

3

Comment

Having written the three letters of apology as instructed, I hope that you have borne in mind four basic criteria, as follows:

1   You followed the instructions given you by your superior. (In real life situation you would not write such a letter unless instructed by your boss.)
2   You expressed yourself with technical and grammatical accuracy.
3   You adopted the tone and approach suited to the type of apology you were making.
4   You read through the completed letters, each time imagining yourself to be the recipient and estimating your reaction to the letter.

It depends upon the efficiency of the company you might work for whether or not you find yourself having to write a large number of letters of apology. It is to be hoped that you do not have to write too many!

Letters of complaint

Although there is an almost infinite variety of causes for complaint in the world of business, you will find that there is not such a variety of styles. The person who instructs you to write a letter of complaint will probably offer only two guidelines as to styles:

1   Write a strong letter of complaint demanding satisfaction or an improvement in standards.
2   Write a mild letter of complaint to ensure that such an error does not happen again.

If the complaint is more serious than 1 then you will probably have the letter dictated to you. If the source of complaint is more trivial than 2 then you will simply hear some grumbling and not be asked to write the letter anyway.

Examples Here are examples of the two types:

1

```
              MicroTec Office Supply

                    16 Warren Avenue
                       ABERSOCH
                        Gwynedd
                        PL10 6KZ
```

                                                    4 July 19--

Macmillan Paper Products Ltd
Cardigan Industrial Estate
CARDIGAN
Dyfed
CD12 6BD

Dear Sirs

    This is the third month running that your delivery has been late in
arriving. Our current order for stationery and ring back folders is
already five days overdue.

    We have a number of valued customers who are being put to some
inconvenience. There seems to be no obvious reason why your normally
prompt deliveries should become so unreliable. I would be obliged if
you would look into this matter as soon as possible.

    Ours is a small, family business in a very parochial area. We
depend very much upon the goodwill of our customers. I am sure you will
appreciate the importance of this matter being cleared up at your
earliest convenience.

        Yours faithfully

        Gwyneth Thomas.

        (Gwyneth Thomas)

2

```
        SPRING HEEL SHOES Ltd
            KESWICK HIGH STREET
                 KESWICK
                 CUMBRIA
                 KK14 7NM
```

                                                    6 October 19--

Cumbria Tannery
Scotland Street
MARYPORT
Cumbria
MP9 8TY

Dear Sirs

        It is unusual and therefore disappointing to have to complain about
the quality of leathers provided to us in an order. It has become clear
that approximately 10 per cent of the calf grade hides in the delivery
of 12 June were below acceptable standard.

        Fortunately an unexpected order for climbing boots was received at
the last minute so we have been able to use the sub-standard hides.

        I am sure that you would wish to be informed of this error in case
other customers are receiving similarly sub-standard products. No doubt
you will see to it that a financial adjustment is made to our next order
to allow for the mistake in quality delivered.

        Yours faithfully

        J. Singh

        (Jany Singh - Production Manager)

It should be fairly obvious which letter is stronger in making its complaint. It should be equally obvious that regardless of the severity of the complaint both letters are firm, controlled and very clear as to the nature of the complaint. There is no loss of temper, threatening language or abuse. As a recipient of either letter you would probably feel that you owed it to the writer to redress the complaint. Contact between the businesses concerned is maintained and improvement will most likely occur.

Assignment

Write two letters of complaint in response to two different situations.

1   You are the personal assistant to the managing director of a small petrol service station and MOT testing station. Your petrol and diesel deliveries have become increasingly unreliable and the pumps actually ran dry for two days last month. You have been asked to write a strong letter of complaint to Arrow Star suggesting that their reliability has become distinctly suspect. Although there is a problem getting petrol suppliers to deliver to small garages, the problem is causing some concern to your boss.

2   You are a clerical assistant in a company that manufactures pickles and sauces. A new label has been designed by a local printer and the first batch of 10 000 has the wrong date printed in the logo. The phrase affected is 'Established 1849' which should read 'Established 1848'. The head of the advertising department for which you work is not very concerned about this minor slip and will accept the current batch of labels. He asks you to write a mild letter of complaint which draws the printer's attention to the discrepancy. The printing firm concerned gives your company particularly favourable rates so you do not want to cause antagonism.

Comment

Having written the two letters of complaint, as requested, you should have ensured that you checked your completed work against the criteria offered for the previous assignments, ie.

1   Have you fulfilled instructions?
2   Is the letter technically accurate?
3   Is the complaint of the appropriate strength?
4   If you imagine yourself as the recipient of the letter, do you believe it to be effective?

Having stressed the importance of getting letters of complaint and apology correctly written, it must be remarked that the writing of such letters is unlikely to be the day-to-day activity of an assistant in the world of business. Such letters will have to be written from time to time and the appropriate tact and diplomacy employed, but there are other sorts of letter. The type that is discussed next may be more representative of everyday work.

Letters requesting information

There are always times when a company will seek information that is not readily available by a phone call, reference book or other form of information retrieval. Somebody will be asked to write a letter to elicit the required information. The somebody could very well be you!

You should ensure that the following points are kept in mind:

1 You must ensure that the request for information is reasonable before you actually write the letter.
2 You must ensure that you use a courteous tone since someone is having to use his time in finding the information you have requested.
3 Your letter must not be ambiguous in any way and the specific requirements should be completely clear.
4 In order to assist the person who receives your letter it is often worth while explaining briefly why you require the information. This is not primarily a courtesy but helps the recipient to understand better the type of information you require.

Examples

Here are two examples of letters requesting information. Notice how the four criteria just mentioned are incorporated without apparent strain into the letters.

Old Salt Cough Products

Cullinshaw Road
St Andrews
Fife
KY9 8HG

11 November 19--

National Maritime Museum
Admiralty Road
Greenwich
LONDON
SE4 7DP

Dear Sir

    I hope you will be so kind as to provide our firm with a small detail of nautical history. Having already done some preliminary research at a local library, we cannot find the information we require and so have turned to you as a final resort.

    We need to know whether a sail powered civilian clipper ship of the same period as <u>Cutty Sark</u> would fly a Union Jack outside territorial waters. Our reason for requesting this information is that we are having a new design of label for our range of cough drops, and the graphic artist employed by ourselves wishes to feature a clipper ship of the period mentioned in full sail on the open sea.

    I hope that you can provide this information and that we are not putting you to much trouble. A SAE is attached for your reply.

        Yours faithfully

        Anne Varley

        (Anne Varley - Clerical Assistant)

King Hadrian's School
Dales Avenue
Bournley
Kent
BD5 9PP

All correspondence to be addressed to The Headmaster

National Motorcycle Scheme
24 Kings Heath
BIRMINGHAM
BH17 5TR

14 April 19--

Dear Sir

King Hadrian's School is a sixth form college catering for the educational need of students in the 16 to 18 year age group.

I have been asked by the headmaster to ascertain whether it is possible for students with motorbikes to receive training in safety and roadcraft from your organization. Ideally we are looking for training to take place two afternoons a week at the school itself.

There is a very large tarmac area close to the school which could be used for practical training and we have county money set aside to fund such a scheme.

If you feel that you would be able to assist us in this venture please send a brochure and an outline of fees and other special requirements. We would hope to start such a project in approximately six months time.

Yours faithfully

Jessica Dixon

(Jessica Dixon - School Secretary)

Comment

You will find, with practice, that by asking yourself four questions every time you have written requesting information you will soon develop a natural, businesslike style.

1 Is this request reasonable?
2 Is this request polite?
3 Is this request clear?
4 Is the background to the request outlined?

Assignment

You are the assistant to the artistic director of a small touring theatre group. It has been decided that in order to cater for the needs of young, school audiences (and ensure a reasonably reliable future!) next year's programme of plays will include two productions that are set texts for pupils in secondary schools studying GCSE English Literature. The artistic director has already discovered that the vast majority of schools in your touring area will be sitting exams organized and administered by the Southern Examinations Board. You are required to write to the secretary of the board and find out what plays will be set for study next year.

Write this letter, bearing in mind the four questions that you should always ask yourself when writing a letter requesting information.

English in use

The split infinitive, homophones, easily confused words

Split infinitive

Splitting the infinitive sounds very painful but is, unfortunately, very easy to do. While not being so noticeable in speech, it is a rather glaring error in the eyes of many readers when encountered on the printed page.

Avoiding the split infinitive is important if you are to give the impression of being a careful and conscientious writer. What the phrase refers to is an easily made mistake when using a verb in its infinitive form (eg: to walk, to care, to decide).

What can happen is that a word or more is placed between 'to' and the 'verb' and then the infinitive has been split. The words that you are most likely to introduce between 'to' and the 'verb' are adverbs. Examples of this bad practice are:

to boldly *go*
to happily *agree*
to skilfully *navigate*

These should be correctly written:

to go boldly
to agree happily
to navigate skilfuly

Obviously in some sentences there may be more than one verb and it is only the infinitive verb that you need to avoid splitting, eg: 'to frequently be singing' is a split infinitive, but 'to be frequently singing' is not a split infinitive as the infinitive here is 'to be'.

Exercise

Rewrite the following sentences so that the infinitive verb is not split.

1　To speedily complete one's work is better than to be lazily apathetic.
2　I prefer to regularly go to the cinema than to go to a disco.
3　The company's policy is to happily and speedily satisfy its customers' requests.
4　A good habit is to always groom your dog's coat carefully.
5　The inspector likes to carefully check the day's production.

Homophones

These are words that have identical sounds when spoken, different meanings and different (although often similar) spellings. It is easy to write down the wrong word when you are writing under some pressure and the effect of such a mistake is often ridiculous when read carefully.

Hare and *hair* are identical in pronunciation but obviously totally different in meaning. 'To comb one's hare' or 'to watch a hair running round a field' would be rather stupid occupations!

Exercise

Write a sentence for each homophone in the following pairs, making sure that you show the difference in meaning clearly, eg:

HAIR   She decided to have her hair cut in a different style.

HARE   They saw a hare being chased by a dog.

ALTER	STAIR	BIRTH	STAKE
ALTAR	STARE	BERTH	STEAK
CEREAL	WRING	BEECH	BORED
SERIAL	RING	BEACH	BOARD
THERE	HERE	WHERE	TO
THEIR	HEAR	WEAR	TWO

If you have some difficulty distinguishing between any of the homophones use a dictionary to check the meanings. You should try to do as many as you can without a dictionary at first.

Words commonly confused

The English language is so rich in variety and has so many borrowings from other languages that there are some words that are very close to each other in spelling and sound but very different in their meaning.

Assignment

Try using the following in individual sentences to show the difference in their meaning. When you have done as many as you can, use a dictionary to check your answers and to complete the sentences you could not manage unaided, eg:

SPACIOUS   The room was airy and spacious with high ceilings.

SPECIOUS   I believed his excuse which seemed quite specious.

ELIGIBLE	FUSSED	DECENT	CONTINUOUS
ILLEGIBLE	FUSED	DESCENT	CONTINUAL
ALTERNATE	UNINTERESTED	CLOTHS	ACCEPT
ALTERNATIVE	DISINTERESTED	CLOTHES	EXCEPT
RESIDENCE	PRINCIPLE	AFFECT	
RESIDENTS	PRINCIPAL	EFFECT	
ADOPTED			
ADAPTED			

14 Ongoing case studies

Honeypot Biscuits

Mrs Jarvis was rather unhappy. In fact she was in a very bad mood indeed. The production line for Honey Crunch Surprise was at a standstill because the supplier of molasses had failed to deliver on time. Although the affected workers had been found work on the Honeywheat line there were shops waiting for deliveries.

Mrs Jarvis had a real problem. Suppliers of high grade molasses were not easily come by and she had managed to agree a good price with the producer in Liverpool, but deliveries had become rather irregular lately. She wanted to keep trading with Mersey Molasses as their product was good, the price right and punctuality of delivery usually good. If deliveries did not return to normal efficiency she would have to consider finding a new supplier. Already two of the retail outlets had telephoned Honeypot Biscuits to enquire why supplies of a fast selling line had become unreliable.

'Sandra, I want you to write a letter of complaint to Mersey Molasses. This just won't do. They've never been as sloppy as this in the past. We're in danger of losing business if we don't get Honey Crunch Surprise production on a regular basis. I phoned last week and got some cock and bull story from an assistant about mechanical problems with their tankers. It's just not on! I reckon old Foster at Mersey Molasses is too tight fisted to get some new tankers. The last vehicle they sent out to us was 20 years old if it was a day. We're one of their best customers and they've been our suppliers for five years but we can't go on like this. Write them a rather strong letter of complaint.'

Sandra thought back to the lessons she had recently attended on letters of complaint. It was quite clear from Mrs Jarvis's tone and instructions that she wanted a strong letter to be written. From what she knew about Honeypot Biscuits it was also clear that Mersey Molasses and its product was important to the quality of their biscuits. What was required was a strong letter that ensured an improvement in deliveries.

Here is the first letter that Sandra wrote:

Mersey Molasses Ltd
Dock Road
Kirkby
LIVERPOOL
LP7 7DS

Dear Sirs

We are extremely disturbed by the terrible record of deliveries of confectionery grade molasses supplied to our company. We have been valued customers for a long time and expect better service than we have been receiving.

Our production lines are at a standstill and profits are going down the drain as local shops are screaming for deliveries. This just isn't on. Unless we have an immediate assurance of 100 per cent reliability of delivery in future, we shall have to seek a new supplier.

We await the favour of a reply at your earliest convenience.

Yours faithfully

(Sandra Kong - Assistant to the Director)

It is a matter of some relief that Sandra decided to redraft the letter! It is a disastrous letter. The only thing that can be said for it is that it is strong. I hope you will realize that there is a difference between a strong letter of complaint and a tirade of abuse. Sandra had clearly forgotten that the letter of complaint was supposed to achieve something positive rather than bring about a breakdown in business relations.

Sandra realized that the letter was inappropriate and decided to start again, bearing in mind the criteria she had learned from her theory lessons.

Assignment

Concentrating on the details of the complaint and avoiding abusive excesses, rewrite Sandra's letter to Mersey Molasses.

Comment

Here is the letter that Sandra finally wrote and which received the approval of Mrs Jarvis. The best comment that can be made is the contrast that emerges when the two letters are read side by side. It is to be hoped that your letter is closer to Sandra's final letter than to her first letter!

HONEYPOT BISCUITS

Haworth Lane
Milham
Lancashire
BB12 9PN

7 October 19--

Mersey Molasses Ltd
Dock Road
Kirkby
LIVERPOOL
LP7 7DS

Dear Sirs

As you will, no doubt, be aware supplies of your confectionery grade molasses to our company have become particularly unreliable of late. It is three months since we have had a delivery on the date agreed.

I am sure you will realize the importance to a manufacturing company such as ours of prompt deliveries of orders on dates agreed. We have no complaint as to the quality of the product but the unreliability of supply is causing difficulties in production as well as losing us the goodwill of our customers.

We would be obliged if you could arrange to investigate the delivery problems we have been experiencing and let us know whether or not there is likely to be a rapid improvement.

Yours faithfully

Sandra Kong

(Sandra Kong - Assistant to the Director)

If you thought carefully about the purpose of this letter of complaint, you will have approximated to Sandra's final letter in tone, if not detail. The letter is strong, without being abusive, consistent in tone and more likely to make the recipient try to remedy the situation rather than sever business relations.

Sandy Bay Leisure Services

Mr Bickerstaffe had yet another problem. Although there was still quite a long time to go before Christmas, it was necessary to ensure that the municipal pantomime would go ahead without a hitch. The weather had been poor during the height of the tourist season and a financial success during the winter season was essential.

A theatre company had been booked some time ago to perform *Robinson Crusoe* over the Christmas season at the Municipal Hall. As there had been some problems in the spring at a rock concert when the electrical circuits of the hall could not cope with the demands of the bands' amplifiers, Mr Bickerstaffe had some concerns about the possible lighting demands.

'Tracy, I'm worried about the electrical circuits at the Municipal Hall. They've been checked by the borough engineer's lads and pronounced safe for normal use but I don't know how much load is going to be demanded by the group doing the panto. You know how it is nowadays with fancy lighting, special effects and all that sort of stuff.

'We don't want to get caught out with overloads and fusing and things like that. The rock festival was a real fiasco and we can't afford to have the customers demanding their money back again.

'Get a letter out to the boss of the company or whoever will know about these things at the theatre group's headquarters. The address and group personnel are on file. Ask them what their requirements are so far as power points, extension cables and so forth are concerned. We don't know what equipment they're bringing with them and what we're expected to provide. Sort it out will you?'

Tracy looked up the information held on file concerning the Touring Theatre of Great Britain. A leaflet showed the following:

Touring Theatre of Great Britain

Address: Helmshore Arts Centre

Funded by: Arts Council of Great Britain

Founded: 1985

Material performed:
Mime, panto, documentary theatre, children's theatre.

Personnel:
Producer – Simon Grange
Artistic Director – Charles Snow
Technical Director – Andy Bryce
Actors – Lyndsey Davies, Clive Rogerson, Tanya Parker, Tracy Reeves, Charlotte Kempson, Alan Dale, Hubert Strange, Will Jackson.

Road Manager – Stephen Wilding

It seemed obvious to Tracy that the Technical Director, Andy Bryce, was the appropriate person to approach with her letter requesting information.

Assignment

Write the letter that you believe it would be appropriate for Tracy to send to Andy Bryce.

You will recall that in the previous chapter four criteria were suggested when writing letters requesting information. These were:

1 The request should be a reasonable one.
2 A courteous tone should be maintained.
3 Ambiguity must be avoided and specific requirements clarified.
4 A brief explanation should be offered showing why the information is required.

Comment

So long as the four 'rules' above were followed you should not have gone too far astray. In order for you to check your version of Tracy's letter it might be useful for you to look at another letter requesting information. In order to be sure that she was writing in an appropriate style, Tracy looked up a letter that her predecessor had written to a visiting dance company the previous year.

SANDY BAY LEISURE SERVICES

THE PROMENADE, SANDY BAY, DORSET, SB15 7CB

10 October 19--

Gazelle Dance Company
Knightsbridge
LONDON
NW3 6GJ

Dear Helen Jenkins

I am writing to you as dance director of Gazelle Dance Company to enquire as to your requirements with regard to flooring at the Municipal Hall.

You have already received details of stage area, wing space and standard lighting arrangements but we have not, as yet received any details concerning your requirements concerning stage surface.

For your information the stage surface is maple wood herring bone blocks over a sprung laminate base. We do have non-skid cushion matting to cover approximately 3/4 of the stage area if this is required.

I should be most obliged if you could inform us whether or not you require the cushion matting to be laid prior to your arrival as it will be necessary to arrange for the caretakers to have this available from the storage rooms.

We are looking forward keenly to your arrival in Sandy Bay and would like to assure you of all the assistance of which we are capable.

Yours sincerely

Edwina Brown.

(Edwina Brown - Assistant to the Director)

---

15 Notices, posters, advertisements, etc

Within organizations it is vitally important to inform and persuade staff on certain occasions. We have seen in Chapter 5 that there are various models for communication routes within organizations. As a general rule the larger and more complex the organization the more important the system of internal communication.

Although a memo can circulate information and requests on a selective basis there is a limit to the efficiency of a 'mass memo'. Once memoranda are used to bring notices to the attention of all the members of an organization the memo ceases to be effective. If this does happen then the staff begin to deal with memos received in a casual manner and this most useful tool of communication becomes devalued.

When a majority of members within an organization would benefit from knowledge of some development or information relating to their work life, then a notice in the form of a bulletin or poster is an important means of communication. There is a whole range of situations where a notice or number of notices is the most effective means of informing a workforce of some relevant development, eg: a change in the company telephone number, the organization of a staff dinner-dance, some aspect of safety procedure at work, a staff training opportunity, etc.

The goodwill and job satisfaction of employees is much more likely to be maintained when there is a relatively open access to information, rather than listening to rumour, gossip or the 'grapevine'. The following examples illustrate and comment on the advantages of alternative methods of general information distribution.

Internal circular notice

M J Rasool
Managing Director
Rasool Electronics

15 May 19--

Dear Colleague

I am pleased to announce that the new face in the quality control area of the assembly shop belongs to Wendy Aspin. Ms Aspin joins us from Careham Electrics where she has worked for five years on data processing systems.

As is your usual custom, I am sure that you will make Ms Aspin feel at home and part of the team. Since the success of our product is based firmly on quality and accuracy of assembly, the presence of extra assistance in the inspection aspect of production can only be of benefit to us all.

We look forward to a happy working relationship with Ms Aspin and wish her well in this settling down period.

Yours faithfully

Mickey Rasool

(Mickey Rasool - MD)

In a small to medium sized organization the arrival of a new employee is likely to affect everyone's work to some extent. The internal circular letter welcoming a new employee serves the purpose of making Wendy Aspin feel part of the group as well as showing the resident workforce that the management recognizes the significance of the workforce's contribution to the success of the business. A notice on a noticeboard would seem too impersonal and is not guaranteed to be read by everyone. In the case of the above internal circular letter a double benefit is achieved in that Ms Aspin is treated as a person of some significance and the recipients of the letter feel that management respects their feelings and efforts.

Notice for display

```
FOR ALL CLERICAL STAFF                    15 Aug 19--

                                          Ref SSS 15/8

REPROGRAPHIC CHANGES ARE HERE AT LAST!

A new leasing policy for reprographic equipment has
meant that the Staff Services Section is at last
able to offer fast and high-quality photocopying
facilities.  It had become obvious that the old
heat-copier and spirit duplicator were past their
prime while the second-hand Minimex photocopier was
being repaired more often than it was working.


Leasing of new equipment and a maintenance contract
means that 'state of the art' reprographic
technology is available now to help you with your
work for the company.
-- But...are you afraid of the new technology?
-- Do you hesitate at using the equipment because of
   the apparently complicated control consoles?
-- Would you like assistance without embarrassment?


Jim Kelly and Tim Bernard are your 'user-friendly'
guides to the new reprographic equipment and will be
holding staff training sessions between 2.00 pm and
3.00 pm each afternoon for the next two weeks in the
Staff Services open office.

Ring them on extension 219 for an appointment or
just drop in between the hours mentioned above.
Remember: the equipment is to help you to help
yourself!
```

This notice, which would be displayed on all relevant notice boards within the organization, is intended to perform three functions:

1 Apologize for the previous low standard of reprographic facilities offered by the Staff Services Section.
2 Advise of the availability of new, high quality equipment.
3 Offer staff training on a voluntary basis for those who might otherwise be overawed or embarrassed by the new technology.

While written in a light-hearted style designed to encourage staff to volunteer for training, the notice contains the required information that it is intended to convey. This is:

1 Those who are eligible to volunteer – 'all clerical staff'.
2 The date on which the notice became effective – '15 Aug 19--'.
3 The main message of the notice – 'staff training sessions'.
4 The time and place where training is available – 'between 2.00 pm and 3.00 pm . . . in the Staff Services open office'.
5 A reference number for possible filing purposes.

Poster for display

ACME STAFF ASSOCIATION
EASTER MONDAY
RAMBLE IN LAKE DISTRICT

AN ENJOYABLE AND LEISURELY
STROLL THROUGH LAKE DISTRICT BEAUTY SPOTS
FRIENDS AND FAMILY WELCOME

LUNCH AND AFTERNOON TEA ARRANGED
AT
LOCAL HOSTELRIES

COACH PICKS UP AT ACME VISITORS' CAR PARK AT 8.00 A.M.
RETURN BY 9.30 P.M.

WATERPROOFS AND SENSIBLE SHOES RECOMMENDED BUT
NO STRENUOUS TRACKS INCLUDED IN RAMBLE.

COST OF COACH AND MEALS £4.75.
BOOK NOW BY CONTACTING YOUR DEPT'S STAFF
ASSOCIATION REPRESENTATIVE OR RING JENNY MITCHELL
ON EXT. 220.

A poster should be eye catching, easy to read and informative. Sometimes posters attempt to cram too much information on to the sheet and the object of the poster is defeated. (The object is to inform and persuade.) Essential information such as time, place and cost is included in the above poster, together with some simple but persuasive wording such as, 'enjoyable and leisurely'. The inclusion of a semi-border pattern and an artist's impression of the beauty spot make the poster pleasing to the eye and likely to stand out from the clutter that noticeboards often attract to themselves.

Advertisement for a newspaper

```
                    J J JONES

               Plumbing Contractors

                  have vacancy for

             part time/possible full time

                    STOREKEEPER

       for checking incoming materials and booking
          out etc, preferably with some knowledge of
      the plumbing trade and with excellent references.

                 Salary by negotiation.

               Apply to: Gareth Jones
           at J J Jones, Plumbing Contractor,
      70 Beach Road, Abersoch, Gwynedd LL52 6TT
```

This is a kind of notice that is *not* for internal communication. An advertisement for inclusion in a local newspaper must include relevant details but also take into account the fact that advertisement rates are often based on a certain cost per word of the advertisement. Very often the newspaper with which you place the advertisement will advise on layout but you should always be certain that the essential information is included. In the example above hardly anything is superfluous. On analysis the following essentials appear:

1   Who is offering the job.
2   What job is offered.
3   Nature of work.
4   Qualifications required.
5   To whom application should be made.

Comment

In the world of work it is highly unlikely that you would be expected to be responsible for writing and designing circular letters, notices, posters and advertisements for newspaper display all on your own. It is likely, however, depending on the size of the organization in which you find yourself employed, that you would be expected to be responsible for one or two of the forms of communication that have been illustrated here.

16 Ongoing case studies

Honeypot Biscuits

'Sandra, I think the time has come to provide some sort of canteen facilities. We're running two shifts now and with winter coming on people are going to get fed up with bringing their own sandwiches and using that old kettle to make themselves a hot drink. I don't want to go at this scheme like a bull at a gate since there will not be much money available as yet for equipment and extensive alterations. I think I'd like to know the staff's feelings about some interim catering provision that they would like to see made available.'

'Would you like me to send a circular letter round the staff, Angela?'

'I don't think that will be necessary, Sandra. A couple of notices will do. One on the wall by the time clock at the entrance and another on that noticeboard by the kettle and sink in the rest room.'

'What sort of notice would you like Angela? What exactly is the announcement?'

'Well I've been thinking about that. It's not so much an announcement – more a notification of a future intention. It's basically a request for ideas and suggestions as to how canteen or refreshment facilities might be organized in the interval before a full canteen can be established. I'd like ideas by word of mouth or in note form via yourself.'

'I'll do a rough draft if you like. It will give you a chance to see if it's all right. I think I understand the kind of thing you want.'

Sandra reached for her pad and made notes of the points she assumed Mrs Jarvis would want including on the notice.

1 Management's realization that refreshment facilities are inadequate.
2 Statement of long-term plans for full canteen facilities.
3 Suggestions/ideas required for short-term improvements that could be made in refreshment facilities while canteen is awaited.
4 Suggestions verbally or in writing to Mrs Jarvis via assistant Sandra Kong.

Since Sandra could not recall any further points required by Mrs Jarvis for inclusion in the notice, she designed the following layout and headline on A4 size paper.

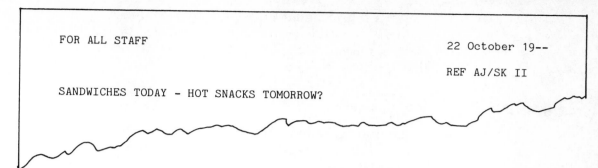

```
FOR ALL STAFF                                    22 October 19--

                                                 REF AJ/SK II

SANDWICHES TODAY - HOT SNACKS TOMORROW?
```

Assignment

Using Sandra's layout, but making a new 'headline', if you wish, instead of the one above, write the notice that you think should be displayed at Honeypot Biscuits. You should use the list of four points that Sandra has already prepared as the basis of your notice.

You will recall that Mrs Jarvis suggested to Sandra that the final notice should be displayed in the rest room and by the time clock at the entrance. Reminding yourself of the departmental organization of Honeypot Biscuits which is outlined in Chapter 6, decide whether you feel there are additional locations where the notice might need to be displayed.

Sandy Bay Leisure Services

'I just can't believe it in this day and age,' complained Mr Bickerstaffe, wearily.' Jobs don't just grow on trees, after all.'

'Perhaps he took offence at the memo,' suggested Tracy.

'There was nothing wrong with the memo Tracy, so don't worry. I hardly think it unreasonable to expect decent standards of appearance and cleanliness. I just had to let Simpkins go after the things he said to Mrs Tulliver.'

'I did hear he was rather rude,' said Tracy, struggling to suppress a smile as she remembered the things that Les Simpkins was supposed to have called Mrs Tulliver, according to the grapevine anyway.

'He was downright obscene! I'm only thankful he's gone before a member of the public was on the receiving end of his abuse.'

'Will he be replaced?' enquired Tracy.

'That's what I've come about Tracy. We'll need a replacement pretty quickly. Let me think. Today's November 4th so we can get an advertisement in the *Sandy Bay Gazette* which comes out on November 7th. Look up Simpkin's job description in the personnel files and draft an advertisement to put in the *Gazette*.'

'What sort of detail should I go into Mr Bickerstaffe?'

'Only what's required. The advertising rates in the *Gazette* have gone up lately. It costs more than a week's salary to put a decent advert in the paper these days. The Finance Officer is not going to welcome any surplus words.'

'What's the deadline for applications, Mr Bickerstaffe?'

'Make it a fortnight after the date of publication. That should allow applicants enough time to respond. Make the advert show that applications are to be made direct to me by the way.'

Assignment

You should:

1 Look at the sample job advertisement which appears in Chapter 15 and also look at the various styles of job advertisements that appear in your local newspaper. Notice the economy of wording used by advertisers.

2 Read the job description that follows shortly and which is the post offered now that the unfortunate Simpkins has been 'sacked'.

3 Read the conversation between Mr Bickerstaffe and Tracy again in order to work out dates for the receipt of applications and the maximum number of words that Tracy may use in the advertisement she must draft.

4 Being as clear and as economical as possible, draft a suitable job advertisement for the 'Situations Vacant' columns of the *Sandy Bay Gazette*.

SANDY BAY LEISURE SERVICES DEPARTMENT

Job Description

TITLE: Library Assistant - with occasional duties as front of house deputy at Library Arts Centre.

DUTIES: Responsibility for receiving returned books and issuing books on loan at main desk of the town library. In addition there will be the responsibility for assisting the front of house manager at arts events taking place in the drama and display studio of the Library Arts Centre.

REQUIRED QUALIFICATIONS: GCSE passes in at least four subjects which must include English and mathematics. Higher qualifications are desirable but not essential.

Patience, a good organizational sense and ability to deal with the general public are personal qualities that are of significant importance in this post.

SALARY/HOURS: The duties of the post mean that a flexi-hours system is worked. An overall total of 40 hours per week is required and salary is according to Municipal Services Clerical Grade One scale.

17 Writing Reports

A report is commonly accepted to be an investigation, in some detail, of a problem, situation or area of choice which includes factual information, findings and conclusions.

Reports vary in their scale and complexity. At one end of the scale is the type of report that is made by a public company secretary for the annual meeting of its shareholders. You will be relieved to know that it is unlikely that you would be asked to prepare a report of such magnitude for some years. At the other end of the scale is a brief, personal response to a situation, such as an accident report. In between these two extremes is a whole range of reports varying in length and required details.

It is probable that the types of report you may be expected to compile will fit into one of three broad categories:

1 *A personal report* in response to a request to provide information on a particular incident or some small area of concern. Such a personal report might be an accident report as previously mentioned.

2 *Routine or progress report* which is in response to a request for updating on developments in some particular area that has previously been the subject of a report. Such a report might involve investigating improvements or deterioration in traffic flow into and out of a factory as a result of new car parking arrangements.

3 *A special or investigation report* which is in response to a request to enquire into a certain matter so that those who have requested the report can come to some decision. The decision may be one that leads to the purchase of a particular product or perhaps leads to a change in practice. Such an investigation report might lead to the purchase of a particular photocopier or lead to a self-service form of catering instead of waitress service.

Although the reports may have different names, purposes and levels of complexity, each has to be undertaken with an awareness of the importance of presentation and layout as well as accuracy of content. Something such as an apparently trivial accident report may become the vital evidence in a possible claim for compensation due to negligence if medical complications develop.

Common practice in the presentation of a written report

1   Reports should have titles and, possibly, a short introduction to the subject under examination as well as a reference to the instructions originally given.
2   Sections should be numbered.
3   If items are listed in the report they should be numbered or lettered.
4   Headings (and subheadings if necessary) should be used in the body of the report.
5   The information should be presented in a logical sequence. This sequence may be chronological or in an order dictated by the subject matter.
6   List your conclusions. (You may also be asked to list your recommendations.)
7   Present the material in an impersonal form. (For example, 'Mr Jones had his cut finger cleaned and a sterilized dressing applied' is impersonal. 'I cleaned Mr Jones's finger and then put an Elastoplast over his cut' is personal.)
8   The report should be written in a professional and neutral manner rather than allowing your feelings to appear. (The reader of your report may suspect the factual basis is weak or biased if you allow your personal prejudice or feelings to show.)
9   Sign and date your report for possible future reference.

Here are two reports which show good and bad practice in the writing and presentation of reports.

Report 1   Safety hazards in central office area

Safety hazards in central office area

FOR   Tony Ashraf – Safety Officer

FROM   Tony Carr – Personal Assistant

16 July 19––

1.0   INTRODUCTION

I was asked on 4 July to prepare a brief report for yourself on actual and potential hazards in the central office area. I was asked to present my initial findings to you by 22 July.

2.0   INFORMATION

2.1   Electrical hazards

Although inspected only six months ago, the power plugs to two of the electric typewriters in the clerical section of the office are cracked across their backs.

The starter to one of the fluorescent tubes in the ceiling lighting is faulty and secretaries regularly stand on a chair to twist the starter to get the tube working.

The main power input to the office photocopier is worn by constant contact with a filing cabinet. The worn area has been mended by being bound with insulation tape.

2.2   Furnishing hazards

Two of the filing cabinets are over 20 years old and often jam shut. They are only capable of being opened by tilting the cabinet backwards and holding the cabinet at an angle while being supported by the foot.

The letter racks for the distribution of incoming mail are secured to the wall by masonry hooks with the exception of the lower left-hand corner where a large dictionary has been placed to support the weight.

2.3 Organizational hazards

In order to maximize use of floor space the secretaries' desks have been arranged so that the door into the office cannot avoid being banged into the first desk on entering unless a small wooden wedge is used to limit the door's arc of movement. The office cleaners often forget to replace this wedge after they have done their early morning clean up.

2.4 Other hazards

Through frequent use, the carpet in front of the letter racks has become very worn. There is a small tear which has already caused a minor accident to a member of the clerical staff (see accident report form filed 9 Feb 19--).

3.0 CONCLUSIONS

3.1 Electrical hazards in the office area are easily rectified without undue expense. There could be hazards that are not yet evident and possibly an electrical inspection could be undertaken in advance of the next scheduled one.

3.2 Furnishing hazards would seem to indicate a need for repair in some instances and purchase of new equipment in others.

3.3 Organizational hazards could be rectified by reorganization of use of space or some mechanical means of limiting the travel of the main door into the office.

3.4 Other hazards are limited to the state of the carpet and replacement of this would seem to be of some urgency. The danger from a worn carpet in close proximity to a somewhat makeshift repair of the letter rack makes this a particularly hazardous area.

REF: TC/JT

Report 2
Secretaries' safety

Secretaries' safety

When you asked me to look into the dangers in the office I thought that there wouldn't be much to report on. When I started looking round and talking to people I was quite amazed. The place is a minefield of dangers wherever you look.

1   Everything is so crowded that people keep bumping into things. The desks are so close together and badly arranged that the door of the office often bangs into the first desk when you go in.

2   The carpet's in a terrible state and someone's going to trip up before too long.

3   A lot of the plugs on the equipment are cracked and could cause a nasty shock if not used carefully.

4   The lead into the photocopier has been repaired by someone so that shouldn't be a problem.

5   The letter rack is in a bad state. I'm told it's been in the office for ages and we could really do with getting a new one.

Suggestion

Some money needs spending before something nasty happens. It really is appalling that our secretarial staff should have to work in such terrible conditions.

It should be immediately clear that Report 1 is infinitely preferable to Report 2. In the second report it is very difficult to distinguish fact from the emotional involvement of the writer. There is little sign of logical arrangement, although the points are numbered. There are few, if any, headings or subheadings to guide the reader through the report. The writer makes some rather vague recommendations (although not asked to do so) and neglects to provide a section on findings.

Comments on Report 1

1 It is clear from the start who has made the report, for whom it is intended, what the instructions were and when the report was assembled.
2 The body of the report lists the relevant information in a logical sequence and divides the information, by the use of subheadings, into a helpful range of categories.
3 The concluding section on the findings made by the compiler of the report provides a useful summary of information as well as guiding the reader towards action that could remedy the most glaring safety hazards revealed.
4 The report is written in a businesslike, unemotional tone and impresses the reader by its objectivity.
5 The writer of the report has fulfilled the requests made with precision and clarity.

Read the two reports again, pretending to be the person who asked for the report to be made. Imagine your reaction.

– Which report is easier to read?
– Which report shows you what needs doing?
– Which report do you trust?

The answers to these questions are, hopefully, obvious.

18 Ongoing case studies

Honeypot Biscuits

With the increasing demand for Honeypot Biscuits' products a late work shift has been established. This shift starts at 4.00 pm and finishes at 11.00 pm. The workers on the shift arrive by public transport which deposits them about three-quarters of a mile from the factory or else they have lifts to work.

A problem is developing over transport home at the end of the shift. Although the workers do not mind the walk from the bus stop in the late afternoon, they are not keen about walking to the bus stop at the end of the shift. Some are considering giving up their work because of the complicated arrangements they are having to make to get lifts home.

Mrs Jarvis has decided, in consultation with her partners, that in order to protect production the firm will try to organize transport home at the end of the shift from the factory itself. Honeypot Biscuits will pay 50 per cent of the cost. The Personnel Manager has worked out that the journey required to deliver the eight workers concerned from the factory to their doors will be approximately 10 miles.

Sandra has been asked to make a report on the cost and availability of transport that could be provided by local firms. Several letters requesting information have been sent out to firms with taxis, minibuses and coaches for hire with driver. Here are copies of the letters that Sandra received in response to her enquiries.

Reply 1

SPEEDY MINICABS

23 Railway Cuttings — Milham — Lancashire — BB11 9PH

Date as postmark

Honeypot Biscuits
Haworth Lane
MILHAM
Lancashire
BB12 9PN

Dear Miss Kong

Thank you for your recent enquiry. We could provide two taxis to take eight people to the addresses in Milham provided by yourself. The cost would be a total of £25.00 per evening.

We should point out that this price would be charged regardless of whether or not the full eight passengers were available for the journey. It may be relevant to your enquiry to add that eight is the maximum number of passengers we could cater for as we will not be purchasing more vehicles in the foreseeable future.

We hope that this information is satisfactory to you.

Yours sincerely

Eric Clopton

(Eric Clopton - Managing Director)

PS I forgot to mention that although one of our vehicles would be available to pick up your workers at 11.00 pm prompt, the other vehicle would not be able to arrive at your premises until 11.15 as it is finishing off another contract at 11.00 pm. I am sure that this will be little, if any, inconvenience.

Reply 2

Hexton Coaches Ltd

Northern Avenue
Milham Industrial Estate
Milham
Lancashire
BB14 7QZ

15 April 19--

Honeypot Biscuits
Haworth Lane
MILHAM
Lancashire
BB12 9PN

Dear Sandra Kong

Many thanks for your request for a quotation for transport. I have pleasure in reporting that we can provide a fourteen seater minibus for the journey outlined at a total cost of £27.00.

I can assure you that your workers would be picked up at 11.00 pm prompt and our driver estimates that the last passenger would be home by 11.30 pm at the latest.

I must add that at the present moment we could not provide transport on Thursdays because of a prior commitment of a long-standing nature. I am pleased to inform you that in a few months' time we will have an additional minibus and driver which will enable us to provide a full service as requested.

I'm sure we can sort out this little Thursday problem.

Yours sincerely

Jack Ambler

(Jack Ambler - Proprietor)

Reply 3

STARLITE TAXIS

3 Hart Street
Milham
Lancs
BB12 9PC

13 April 19--

Honeypot Biscuits
Haworth Lane
Milham
Lancs
BB12 9PN

Dear Ms Kong,

I have pleasure to respond to your request for transport as outlined in your letter received this morning.

We can provide a twelve-seater mini-coach, with driver, for a total of £26.00.

I hope that this will prove satisfactory to your director.

Yours sincerely,

Alice Trubshaw

Alice Trubshaw
Secretary to Director

Reply 4

EXECUTIVE LINE COACHES LTD

Milham Road
Milham
Lancashire
BB9 7YF

16 April 19--

Honeypot Biscuits
Haworth Lane
MILHAM
Lancashire
BB12 9PN

Dear Sirs

In response to your request for quotation regarding late night transport. I am pleased to report that we have a 44 seater luxury coach available.

All our coaches have reclining seats, tables, toilet facilities and video as well as air conditioning as standard.

The cost would be £35.00 and we look forward to confirmation of acceptance. Assuring you of our best attention at all times.

Yours faithfully

Adrian Brinks

(Adrian Brinks - Transport Manager)

Reply 5

FRanks Motors
Gasworks Lane
Milham
Lancs

Dear Homeypot Biscuits

I got your letter c ouple of days ago about the lift some of your workers need late at night. I"m a bit late in replying eeause I lost your letter but its turned up now.

I've got a roomy Ford transit van available. It's not got any windows xxxxxxxx but at that time of night your people won 't want to be looking out at the sights, will they.

There's lotsof room and you can squeeze in a dozen at a pinch. I could do the run for you most nights for £10 cash. Nowand again I might not be to make it dead on time as I lend the van to a local farmer on Market Days. He usuually gets it back in good time.

Let me know when youd like me to start.

Yours

Reply 6

Lochinvar Taxis
Gisburn Road
Milham
Lancashire
BG17 5TF

15 April 19--

Honeypot Biscuits
Haworth Lane
MILHAM
Lancashire
BB12 9PN

Dear Sirs

Thank you for your request for a quotation to provide regular transportation from your factory to the addresses you attached to the request.

I am pleased to report that we could provide two taxis (together accommodating 10 persons) on a regular basis for a total of £24.00.

I must add, however, that we would require a six month contract renewable at reasonable rates dependent on rises in fuel costs.

Trusting that this will meet your requirements, I look forward to receiving your confirmation.

Yours faithfully

Stuart Evans

(Stuart Evans - Director)

Three firms have not replied, even though it is over a week since the letters requesting information were sent out by first class mail.

Assignment

With the information you have to hand in the letters of reply, write the report that Sandra has been requested to present to Angela Jarvis. Remember to refer back to the nine criteria for presenting a written report which were outlined in the previous chapter. You should also look back at the better of the two 'hazard reports' that appeared in the same chapter.

Comment

You will have realized that some of the replies are less than businesslike in their presentation. For example, a business letter never contains a PS (although a computer generated circular might).

Sandy Bay Leisure Services

Mr Bickerstaffe has received a memo from Mrs Evans, the staff catering organizer, in which she comments on the increasing demand for hot snacks she is receiving from users of the central staff canteen at mid-morning and mid-afternoon breaks.

It appears that the gas stoves and equipment currently in use mean that it takes a considerable time to heat pies and similar foods when requested at short notice. Since staff movements to different Leisure Services sites make it impossible to assess accurately demand for hot snacks, a problem has arisen. If the current kitchen equipment is used to heat up snacks in advance of the breaks, quite a lot of food wastage occurs. If snacks are heated up on demand, the short break is almost over before the food is ready. Mrs Evans has suggested that a microwave oven be purchased but she has little knowledge of prices or models.

Mr Bickerstaffe can see the advantage of purchasing a microwave oven for the canteen's use. Financial turnover may well increase and the efficiency of the service and lowering of waste also appeal. Staff and workers will have less excuse to take unofficial 'extended breaks' in the canteen if the service is quicker and more efficient.

'Tracy, I'm very tempted by the idea of purchasing a microwave oven for Mrs Evans at the central canteen. You've seen her memo and it makes a lot of sense. I'd like you to do me a short report on the models available that might be suitable. I can probably find £500 from the capital equipment budget although something that is appropriate and less expensive wold be very acceptable. Please get me a report with your personal recommendations by Friday.'

A number of phone calls and a visit to the main shopping centre of Sandy Bay at lunchtime resulted in a shortlist of available microwaves. Tracy adjusted her list as a result of checking in the local library an independent consumer magazine that had recently tested microwave ovens.

She discovered that microwave ovens come into three classifications:

1 *'Compact microwaves'* in the price range £200 to £300. These have a small capacity, consume little power, are easy to operate but are slower to heat food than more powerful models.
2 *'Standard microwaves'* in the price range £300 to £400. These have a large oven, consume more power than compact models but are quicker to heat food. They take up quite a lot of space but not significantly more than a compact model.
3 *'High-technology microwaves'* in the price range £450 to £950, These have high power and slightly faster food heating times than standard microwaves. They have highly sophisticated controls and gadgets. (According to the consumer magazine these controls and gadgets confuse many users.) Their oven size is invariably the same as 'standard microwaves'.

Tracy found the following models available locally in each of the three categories:

Compact microwave

Sanchuni Mini-Wave 100   Capable of being wall mounted to save space – only one power setting – smallest oven space of all models – simple controls – £190.00 in local electronic retailer's sale – one year guarantee.

Proteus Micro 2000   Free standing – two power settings – average oven space for category – simple controls – £225.00 in local hypermarket – manufacturer recently went out of business – six months guarantee.

Electron Micro-Superior   Wall mounted or free standing – average oven space for category – simple controls – two power settings – comes with free set of cutlery – £270.00 in local electrical goods wholesale warehouse – one year guarantee.

Standard microwaves

Sonic-Cook MC225   Free standing – cannot be wall mounted – several power settngs – good sized oven for category – simple to use electronic controls – senses automatically when food is ready – warning bell to signal food ready – £360.00 in local hypermarket – two year guarantee.

Tri-Wave K625   Free standing or wall mounted – several power settings – good sized oven – simple electronic controls – warning bell and automatic timer – £359.00 in local electrical goods wholesale warehouse – six month guarantee – five year parts and labour insurance obtainable for a single payment of £30.00. (A shop soiled model as above is available for £320.00 with same guarantee and insurance deal available.)

Simplex Mode 3000   Free standing or wall mounted – several power settings – complicated controls – good sized oven – warning bell and automatic timer – available in choices of ten different colours – £140.00 in local electronic retailer's sale (normally listed at £445.00) – one year guarantee.

High technology microwaves

Prince Micro Z 1100   Free standing – cannot be wall mounted – several power settings – extremely complicated controls – very fast cooking and heating times – automatic warning bell indicates food is ready – available in six different colours – £445.00 in local electrical goods wholesale warehouse – one year guarantee – five year parts and labour insurance available for single payment of £35.00.

Data Tec QL 1100   Exactly the same model as above but assembled in Britain – three colour options available – £445.00 in local hypermarket – two year guarantee – (one shop soiled model is available for £435.00).

Assignment

Using the information above, write Tracy's report for Mr Bickerstaffe. Remember that he wanted her to include her personal recommendations in the report and these should be placed at the end of the 'conclusions' section with a new subheading. Look back at Chapter 17 before you start, in order to remind yourself of the required layout.

19 The use of a library and index systems

Libraries have been changing rapidly over the last few years. Attitudes to the role they play in the community and the services they provide have altered and the general image of serious-minded stuffiness has disappeared. Libraries are still places for serious study and research but they are also lively and entertaining centres for community activities and displays. Modern technology and a more flexible attitude to information storage and retrieval have altered the atmosphere and services of libraries.

Use of a library

Despite developments that may have been made in presentation, the heart of a library remains its fund of information. The majority of this information is still stored in books but the following sources of information will be found in most reasonably up-to-date libraries:

1   *Books*   Most categories in the broad divisions of non-fiction and fiction will be found as well as reference collections including: dictionaries, encyclopedias, manuals and directories.
2   *Audio-visual*   Sound cassette tapes, slides, film strips, video tapes and micro-film records.
3   *Journals and magazines*   General and specialist journals covering a wide range of topics.
4   *Topic files*   Clippings from feature articles and newspapers arranged under headings of popular and frequently requested topics.

The above are sources of information available within your library on demand. The scale of information available will vary according to the size of your local library. However, it would be a mistake to believe that the potential resources of information are limited by its size and financial resources. Since the public library service is national in its organization, any library can provide, on request, the millions of books and journal articles available throughout the country. This service is available through the following routes:

Inter-library loans   If the desired source of information is not found on the shelves or in the index system of your local library, the staff will arrange to borrow the required source from other libraries in the country. The library staff are always available to help you to find the information you require, even if it is not immediately available.

It is always possible that you are not aware of titles or sources available in researching the particular area of enquiry. In this case, if the time element is not pressing, the following can be of help:

BIROS

This is not a reference to ball point pens but the initials of an extremely useful service offered by most libraries. The initials stand for: Bibliographic Information Retrieval On-line Service. This impressive sounding service is a computerized information retrieval system which is linked to data bases all over the world and will, on request, provide detailed bibliographies on a wide range of subjects.

For example, you have been asked to provide some background information on William Morris and his fabric designs. By approaching the library staff with details of your requirements they will help you by putting the BIROS system into operation. What you will receive is a list of authors, titles and publishers of books and journals dealing with William Morris and particularly his work on fabric designs. It is up to you then to decide which books you will require to help you in your task.

Finding your way through the library

It is all very well to know, in theory, what is available in a library. It is almost equally important to understand how to find the material that you require. Librarians will always try to give you help but they are busy people and basic knowledge of how the shelves of a library are organized will save the librarians and *you* quite a lot of time.

The library index system

Everything in the library is logically arranged. The most common system of organizing or categorizing material is the Dewey Decimal method. This involves all material being given a particular number based on the subject category.

000 – General works, encyclopaedias, etc
100 – Philosophy, psychology
200 – Religion
300 – Social sciences
400 – Languages
500 – Pure science
600 – Technology, applied science
700 – Arts, crafts, recreations
800 – Literature
900 – History, geography, biography

Books on the shelves will be arranged in sections according to the broad category range to which the library staff have assigned them following the Dewey Decimal scheme. Books on technology, for example, will be found on the shelves carrying numbers in the range 600 to 699. The individual number will be found on the spine of each book for ease of checking. If you know the particular Dewey Decimal number of the book you require it will not take you long to find the 600 section of shelving and then the particular area of the shelf you require.

It is highly unlikely, however, that you will be carrying round in your head the reference number or even the category of the book you require. In order to find the Dewey Decimal of the book you want or to discover what books are available in the topic area you require, the following choice of index systems is available in the library:

Subject index

Everything in the library has its own Dewey Decimal number as has been said. Every subject has its own special number. To find out what number has been given to your subject check the subject index. Here the cards are filed A–Z by subject.

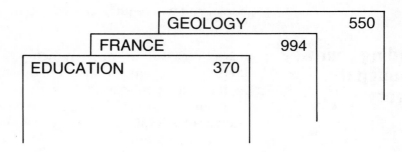

Classified index

Once you have discovered the number for your subject you could go straight to the shelf. By doing this you will miss books that are out on loan and also audio visual material which is housed separately. For a complete list of the library's stock on a particular subject look in the classified index. Here the cards are filed in number order.

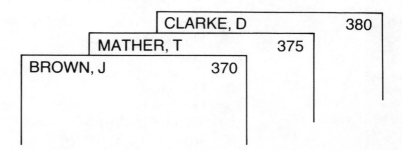

Name/title index

The name/title index lists books by author's surname and the title of the book. As always, the Dewey class number is given in the top right-hand corner of each card.

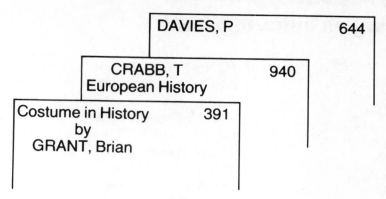

Books by and about a person are also listed together in this section of the catalogue.

The simplified model shown in Figure 19.1 may help you to find your way around a library when searching out sources of information.

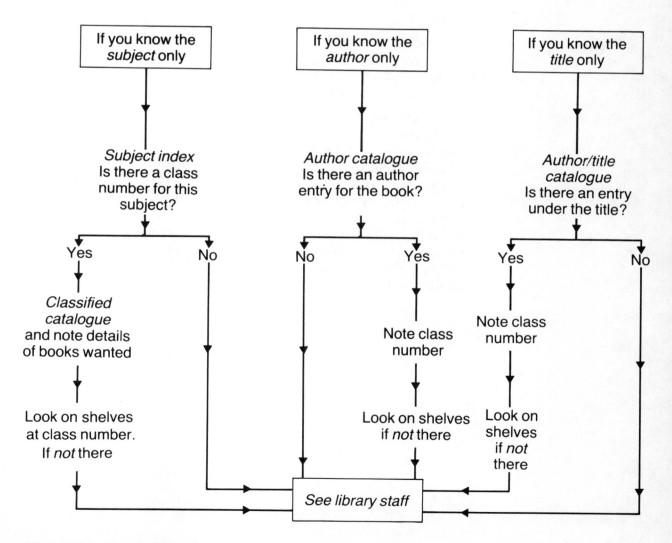

Figure 19.1   How to find a book

Using an index in a book

Having found the book or other source of information that is required it remains to find the particular information without reading the material from beginning to end. In the case of a book the problem is considerably eased by the presence of a contents list at the front of the text or an index at the back of the text.

The contents page or pages may vary considerably in detail. You may simply find some chapter headings with page numbers or you may find that a brief synopsis of the contents of each chapter is also included. This may be sufficient for your needs. All you need to do then is to turn to the relevant chapters and find your information.

It may be that the contents pages do not meet your requirements, in which case the index at the back of the book should be of help. A typical index is organized alphabetically and by each entry you will find the page numbers in the book which contain a reference to the particular entry. The entry could be under a person's name, the name of a place or event or a topic.

A typical entry might be as follows:

World War One:
    causes, 98–119, 150, 176, 188–197, 202
    treaties, 34–40, 111, 207–219

This tells the reader that references to the causes of the First World War will be found on the pages referred to and particular emphasis on this topic between pages 98 and 119 as well as between pages 188 and 197. References to treaties concerning the war will be found on the pages numbered as well as particular emphasis between pages 34 and 40 and between 207 and 219.

Ultimately the best way to familiarize yourself with the facilities of a library, its organization and indexing systems, together with the indexing of individual books, is to spend some time in a school, college or municipal library. Librarians may be very busy people but they are also very helpful.

20 Ongoing case studies

Honeypot Biscuits

The company was in a state of some excitement. After a previous meeting at a trade fair, Mr Mulanga Piri was to visit Mrs Jarvis at Honeypot Biscuits to inspect the plant and discuss a possible contract to supply Mr Piri's trading stores in the African republic of Zambia.

'This could be a very valuable connection, Sandra. The Piri group of stores is established thoughout Zambia apparently and if we can settle on a competitive wholesale price, allowing for the transport costs, then we'll be in a very strong position.' Mrs Jarvis frowned and looked thoughtful.

'I know that he's also paying a visit to York and Co Confectionery the day before he comes here to look at our plant and talk business. I reckon one of us will get the contract. I wish we had an edge on York and Co.'

'He's bound to be impressed by the factory, Angela. I know I was when I first came here.'

'That's all very well Sandra, but we need to have some sort of edge over our rivals.'

'Perhaps if we hung the Zambian flag over the entrance?'

'That's not a bad idea Sandra! In fact I think Mr Mulanga Piri might be rather impressed if we did our homework and showed how much we know about the country where we hope our products are going to be on sale.'

'I'll see what I can find out shall I?'

'Yes please, Sandra. Get me some notes on Zambia as soon as you can. Climate, size, population, geography – that sort of thing.'

Sandra thought back to her lessons at college on synthesizing information from a variety of sources. She noted down the potential sources of facts on Zambia: (a) atlas (b) library (c) encyclopaedia (d) travel agent.

After a few more moments' thought she added (e) people and (f) telephone directory.

Atlas   This confirmed what Sandra vaguely remembered from school geography lessons. Zambia lies south of the Equator in the tropical belt of Africa. It has no sea coast and is about 5000 miles from Britain.

Library/encyclopaedia   Use of the index at the local library revealed a number of specialist books on central Africa as well as some interesting background information in the relevant volume of a set of encyclopaedias in the reference section. She noted down details of population, climate, recent history, transport systems and industry as well as the address of the Zambian High Commission in London.

Travel agent A visit to the local travel agent did not reveal much more information than she had already gained from an hour in the library. However, she did discover some up-to-date facts concerning freight and passenger routes to Zambia.

Telephone directory/people Remembering that a near neighbour had been to Zambia on a safari holiday the previous summer, Sandra looked up his telephone number and got some impressions of the country from a recent visitor. She also looked up the number of Zambian High Commission in London and made contact with a helpful secretary who gave Sandra some information on Mr Mulanga Piri and his chain of stores in Zambia.

Realizing that Mrs Jarvis only wanted a summary of relevant information, Sandra made a synthesis of information that might be useful to know before Mr Piri's arrival.

```
                             ZAMBIA
```

Background

The old colony of Northern Rhodesia gained its independence from Britain in 1964 and became the republic of Zambia under President Kenneth Kaunda, who is still the head of state. Zambia is a member of the British Commonwealth.

The country

The area of Zambia is about four times that of the British Isles. The population is approximately 7 million, composed mainly of Africans with some Asians and Europeans. The climate is sub-tropical with a rainy season between March and August and a dry season for the rest of the year. The main source of income is copper and other minerals, which are mined in the north, and agriculture over the rest of the country (maize, tobacco and sugar cane). There is some tourism with game parks and the Victoria Falls being the main centres.

Transport

A rail line runs from the north to the south of Zambia with access into Zimbabwe and southern Africa. The road system is in poor condition, although a paved road does run in roughly the same area as the line of rail. The rest of the country has dirt roads which can be difficult in the rainy season. There is an international airport at Lusaka, which is the capital of Zambia.

Commercial life

Many of the commercial retail outlets are run by Asians, although there is a growing number of African businessmen of which Mr Mulanga Piri is a good example. Mr Piri was the first Zambian to graduate from the London School of Economics and after a career in the civil service established a chain of retail supply stores in all the main towns along the line of rail (Ndola, Kitwe, Broken Hill, Lusaka, Monze, Livingstone).

Miscellaneous

The country is divided into four provinces: Northern, Southern, Eastern and Western. The national flag is green, black and red stripes with an eagle emblem. Zambia seems to be politically stable and the standard of living, compared to many African countries, is reasonably high.

Imports

Imports into Zambia can take a long time by sea and road. Goods that are sent by sea are shipped out to either Mozambique or Capetown in South Africa. This is followed by a long and sometimes unreliable system of road or rail transport to Zambia. Air freight is much more reliable and quicker but more expensive.

Assignment

Assume that you have a similar task to that which Sandra has to perform in preparing a brief background of the country from which an important visitor is to arrive. Select *one* of the following countries or areas as the object of general research similar in scope to that which appears above for Zambia.

Yugoslavia *or* Cyprus *or* Western Australia *or* Singapore *or* British Columbia (Canada).

Sandy Bay Leisure Services

Next year will be the centenary of Sandy Bay's establishment as a borough. Effectively this means that it is the town's hundredth birthday. The Leisure Services Department is planning to issue a small booklet to be available for sale in libraries, local bookshops and tourist information offices.

'Tracy, I'm up to my eyes with more pressing work at the moment. The booklet doesn't come out until next Easter but a printer is going to want copy and illustrations by Christmas or January at the latest. I can't afford the time to root out all the sources of information.'

'So you'd like me to do some preliminary research?'

'Bless you Tracy. I don't like to ask this but I am very busy for the next few days. I don't want you to write any copy, just make me a list of books and other sources that I can refer to later when putting the booklet together.'

Tracy sighed and reached for a telephone directory. Mr Bickerstaffe was certainly a busy man but he did know how to delegate. A few phone calls later and Tracy had a basic list of general sources which might prove useful in her search for Mr Bickerstaffe's general material.

Here are her notes:

People The head of history at the local high school is something of an enthusiast in the study of local history.

The owner of a local bookshop that specializes in old books and maps may be of use.

A local author who some years previously wrote and had published a small volume on Sandy Bay between the two World Wars may be worth contacting.

<u>Library</u> The central library of Sandy Bay has all the copies of the <u>Sandy Bay Gazette</u> for the last 90 years on microfilm.

There are a number of books on the history of the county which, according to the index in the back of each, contain sections or whole chapters on Sandy Bay.

<u>Reference works</u> The current copy of <u>The Writers' and Artists' Yearbook</u> lists the name and address of the Sandy Bay Photographic Society. A telephone call to the secretary revealed that two local amateur photographers have a collection of Victorian photographs of the local area.

Assignment

Assume that *your* town or city is celebrating the anniversary of its establishment. Find out what sources of written and visual information are available in your district. Make a list under general source headings as Tracy did for Mr Bickerstaffe. In *your* list give names, addresses, telephone numbers, titles, index numbers, etc.

21 Interpretation and design of pie charts and bar graphs

Words versus 'pictures'

There comes a time in the communication process when words on their own need some assistance. If you were trying to describe the processes involved in tying a knot or giving instructions where to find a particular building in a city, a diagram or map would probably be more effective in conveying the information than a paragraph or more of words.

There are a number of reasons why the written or spoken word fails in certain circumstances and the diagram or chart has greater accessibility:

1 Sentences are constructed in such a way that it is not until the end has been reached that the sense is totally clear. It might take a number of sentences actually to convey a fairly simple instruction or process. The diagram allows an almost instant impression of the totality of the function being illustrated, eg: a sales graph for the year would be much quicker and easier to take in than a paragraph or more of exposition.

2 Complicated procedures or shapes are quickly illustrated by diagrams whereas words can easily become confusing and repetitive, eg: a diagram to demonstrate why the shape of an aeroplane wing generates 'lift' is more easily comprehended than the equivalent description in words (see Figure 21.1).

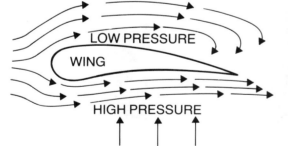

Speed of the air over the upper surface of a suitably shaped wing is greater than the wind speed while the air passing the lower surface is slowed down. The result of these differences in the speed of the air is that the air pressure on the upper surface is decreased and that on the lower surface is increased. Since the pressure on the lower surface is greater than the pressure on the upper surface the wing will be subjected to an upward force. This force is called 'lift'.

Figure 21.1   Why the shape of an aeroplane wing generates lift

3 Proximity and relationships are often difficult or tedious to demonstrate by the use of words on their own, eg: the organization and placing of equipment in an office or instructions for putting together a 'flat-pack' kitchen cupboard are simply and unambiguously demonstrated by diagrams or plans. The same information in words would need constant re-checking in order to keep the overall picture in mind.

111

4   Diagrams and charts are virtually international in their ability to be interpreted. Language is often very regional in a world sense. Although English or French or Spanish may be fairly widely used in certain areas of the world, it is only diagrams or charts that are truly international.

Graphs

These are non-verbal diagrams with which most people will be familiar in one form or another. In real life and cartoons they seem to figure prominently at the end of hospital beds showing temperature and pulse rate. They also feature on board room walls, showing sales figures soaring or plummeting. In real life or cartoons, sudden variations are very obvious and a probable cause for elation or alarm.

The principle behind graphs is that a changing variable is charted against a fixed variable. The classic example is a sales graph where the sales (a changing variable) are charted against the months of the year (a fixed variable).

Figure 21.2 is a simple line graph to illustrate the sales of ice cream cornets by a manufacturer over a 12-month period.

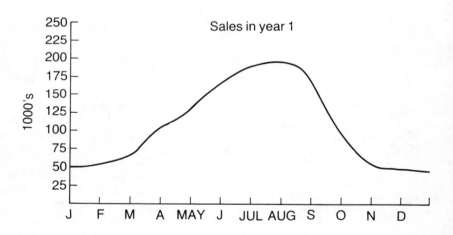

Figure 21.2   Sales of Ice cream cornets over a 12-month period

The graph quickly demonstrates the rise and fall of sales over a 12-month period. By checking the sales figure on the left-hand vertical line against the lower horizontal line which shows the months of the year, it is easy to see the following developments:

1   The figures for November, December, January, February and March are fairly static with sales of around 50 000 per month.
2   Sales start to rise in April and May.
3   Sales are at their highest in June, July, August and September.
4   Sales start to dip quite severely in October.

The line graph (Figure 21.3) shows sales for the following year. By comparing the two graphs it is possible to make a number of observations as well as compare sales figures.

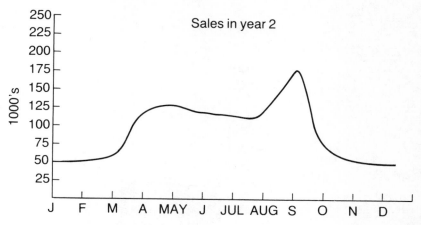

Figure 21.3   Sales for the year after the figures given in Figure 21.2

The following conclusions (or reasonable guesses) might be made on comparing the two graphs:

1   The sales of ice cream do not vary much in winter from year to year.
2   The rise in April and May is comparable with the previous year, with sales slightly higher in each month.
3   Sales during the summer months of the year dip surprisingly which may be put down to poor weather unless there are other reasons such as a breakdown in supplies or strike action among the workforce.
4   There is a return to healthier sales in September which might be due to an improvement in weather in the autumn of the year.

The comparison of such line graphs is made easier if the two are merged together. Such a composite line graph for the two sets of sales figures just illustrated would appear as shown in Figure 21.4.

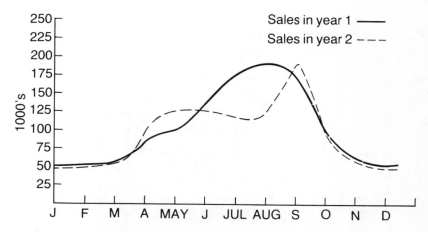

Figure 21.4   Composite line graph of Figures 21.2 and 21.3

As an alternative to the traditional line graph, with its rising and falling curve, the bar graph variation shown in Figure 21.5 is held by some people as more easily and quickly interpreted.

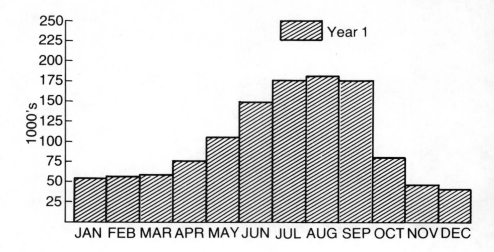

Figure 21.5   Bar graph

Figure 21.5 depicts the same information as the first line graph for ice cream sales. The solid blocking of the sales for each month gives a stronger visual impression of the differences and changes from month to month of sales.

Just as the figures for two years' sales were included in composite form for easier comparison, a bar graph can depict the equivalent information for a similar two-year period (Figure 21.6).

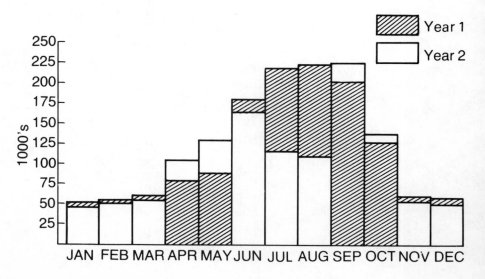

Figure 21.6   Bar graph of years 1 and 2

Pie charts

There are times when it is desirable to show how component parts go to make up a whole and the relative proportions of these parts. In this case a pie chart is often useful. This is simply a diagram that shows the whole as a circular pie and the parts that are being compared are different sized slices of the pie (Figure 21.7).

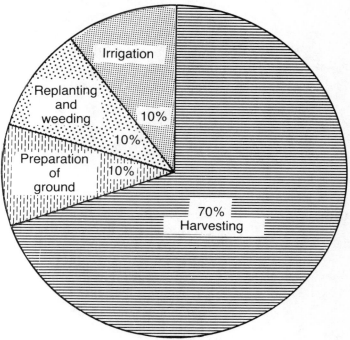

Figure 21.7   Labour requirements of sugar cane production

The relatively simple pie chart (Figure 21.7) shows how the labour requirements of sugar cane production are divided into four activities in a year. The interpretation of a pie chart is fairly easy. This chart shows:

10 per cent of the labour time is spent in *preparation of the ground*.
10 per cent of the time is spent in *replanting and weeding*.
10 per cent of the time is spent in *irrigation*.
70 per cent of the time is spent in *harvesting*.

In designing a pie chart to present factual information one has to be aware of some simple mathematical facts.

1   The circle (or pie) has 360°.
2   The total presented within the pie is 100 per cent.
3   The above two facts mean that 1 per cent of the total will equal 3.6° of the circle (360 ÷ 100 = 3.6°).
4   Therefore if you wish to indicate a 10 per cent slice of the pie (as in 'preparation of ground' in the pie chart for sugar cane production) your slice should take up 36° of the circle (10 × 3.6 = 36).

Exercise

Draw a pie chart to depict the following proportions:

25 per cent of an average person's day is spent sleeping.
25 per cent of an average person's day is spent in leisure.
50 per cent of an average person's day is spent working.

Comment

You may have recognized that the simple percentages given in the above exercise did not need mathematical calculation since each 25 per cent slice would take up a *quarter* of your pie and a 50 per cent slice would take up the remaining *half* of your pie.

Since statistics are very seldom so easy or neat as the above, the calculations would have to be worked out in advance before dividing up the pie. For the simplified figures of the exercise you would have calculated as follows:

sleeping = $25 \times 3.6° = 90°$
leisure $= 25 \times 3.6° = 90°$
working $= 50 \times 3.6° = \underline{180°}$

$$360° \text{ total pie}$$

Exercise

Design a pie chart to illustrate the specified proportions. Production of tin ore in the world last year was in the following percentages: Malaysia 33, Bolivia 14, USSR 12, China 12, Thailand 7, Indonesia 7 and other countries 15 per cent.

The advantages of a pie chart lie in its instant visual impact and easy comprehension of proportion. Problems can arise when too many slices have to be represented. For most people a pie chart ceases to be useful once the circle has been divided over ten times.

Pie charts and bar graphs are tools to assist the written or spoken work when communicating. They do not replace words. A combination of words and diagrams will, in certain circumstances, permit more accurate and successful communication than words or diagrams alone.

English in use

Further summary work

In Chapter 9 advice and demonstration was given concerning methods and systems of précis writing. Read the following passage and make a summary in about 125 words. You may wish to remind yourself of the techniques available by looking again at the relevant parts of Chapter 9.

The Chairman's annual report

In presenting the balance sheet for the financial year just ended, your directors and I are pleased to report another increase in net profit and a healthy improvement in turnover. This outcome is even more pleasing in that this year has seen a continuation of our policy of re-equipping the administration and accounts departments with up-to-date electronic equipment to facilitate the continued smooth running of our operation. You will see from the balance sheet that replacement costs have been high but this should not cause alarm as sales have continued to rise at a rate ahead of that of our competitors and we have been assured by management consultants that no new equipment should be required for at least five years.

Sales in Europe have expanded, although trading with traditional markets in Commonwealth countries has continued a slow but steady decline. So long as interest rates remain under control and there is no significant increase in energy costs in the forthcoming year, we are confident that the profits from new European markets will help us to maintain our strong financial position.

It is a source of some regret that our trading position in the home market has not increased as expected. Our main market rivals unveiled a new range of products in the middle of the year and for a time our sales' curve dipped as a consequence. Figures for the last two months show our product reasserting itself in British High Street sales and there is reason to hope that when the market stabilizes we will emerge as the leader once again.

Rationalization of staffing has meant that the workforce shrank by 4% in the last year while output expanded by 17%. Much of the credit for this increase in efficiency must be put down to the steady investment made in new production equipment over the past three years.

In times of rapid change and development it would be a brave man who could forecast our company's position in a year's time. I would say, however, that so long as we continue to supply traditional quality goods made on up-to-date equipment by a loyal and dedicated workforce we stand a very good chance of doing even better business in world markets in the coming year.

(375 words)

Comment

When writing your summary bear the reader in mind. A summary of a piece such as that above is the kind of thing which would appear as a small article in a newspaper or magazine. Imagine your reader as having a general but not specialized interest in the report to be summarized.

22 Ongoing case studies

Sandy Bay Leisure Services

'Tracy, I've just had an idea!'

Tracy struggled to avoid sniggering. It wasn't that Mr Bickerstaffe was short of ideas; in fact he was full of ideas. The problem was that Mr Bickerstaffe's ideas often involved Tracy in doing quite a lot of basic work to bring the ideas into reality.

'Really, Arthur?'

'Yes, I was just glancing at a holiday brochure for France and was quite surprised at the sunshine and temperature statistics they were quoting for Brittany and Normandy.'

'I see,' said Tracy, half realizing what was going to come next.

Yes, The holiday firm concerned was contrasting the sunshine and temperature figures for London and St Malo over a 12-month period. I must say the figures looked quite impressive.'

'But our brochure for next season is already at the printers isn't it?'

'Exactly. I'm thinking about the brochure after that. The county is always going on about this being the sunshine coast of Britain. Let's put Sandy Bay on the meteorological map, Tracy.'

'Would you like me to get some figures together?'

'Would you? That's very kind, Tracy. Let's see how Sandy Bay compares with London for sunshine and temperature.'

'Do you want the figures for a 12-month period, Arthur?'

'Yes, let's see what they look like. And do you think you could put them together in some sort of visual form so readers can quickly see the climate advantages of Sandy Bay?'

'Would a couple of composite bar graphs be appropriate?'

'Why . . . yes, yes, I think that would do nicely, Tracy.'

Assignment

Table 22.1 gives the average sunshine hours per day for each month of the year for Sandy Bay and London. Tracy found the information in an atlas in the reference section of the local library. Design a composite bar graph to depict these figures. You may wish to refer to the examples given in the previous chapter.

Table 22.2 gives the average temperature figures for each month of the year for Sandy Bay and London. Tracy found the information from the same source as the previous statistics. Design a composite bar graph for displaying the contrast in these figures.

For either of these bar graphs you may wish to use two colours or pattern filling in order to make the contrast between Sandy Bay and London clear.

Table 22.1 **Average hours of sunshine per day for each month of the year**

Sandy Bay		London	
Jan	2.5	Jan	2.0
Feb	3.5	Feb	3.0
March	4.0	March	3.5
Apr	6.5	Apr	5.5
May	8.0	May	6.5
June	11.0	June	8.5
July	10.5	July	7.0
Aug	8.5	Aug	7.0
Sept	6.0	Sept	5.5
Oct	4.0	Oct	3.0
Nov	2.5	Nov	2.0
Dec	2.0	Dec	1.5

Table 22.2 **Average daytime temperatures (°C) for each month of the year**

Sandy Bay		London	
Jan	7.5	Jan	5.5
Feb	7.5	Feb	5.0
March	9.5	March	7.5
Apr	11.5	Apr	10.0
May	15.0	May	12.0
June	18.0	June	17.0
July	21.5	July	19.0
Aug	21.0	Aug	18.5
Sept	17.5	Sept	16.0
Oct	14.5	Oct	13.0
Nov	12.0	Nov	9.0
Dec	9.0	Dec	7.0

Honeypot Biscuits

'Sandra, I've had some statistics from the sales and production sections referring to production figures and market research statistics from a national survey (see Figures 22.1–22.3). I want to do a report for the section leaders' meeting on Friday and could do with a breakdown of the graphs and diagrams by tomorrow.'

'How would you like the material presented, Angela?'

'Oh, nothing too elaborate. Try to give me a paragraph summary of what each graph or diagram shows. I'll be giving out copies of the original material. I just want a few notes on what the statistical material suggests so I can save the time of ploughing through everything in detail.'

'So a paragraph or so with headings for each diagram will do?'

'Yes, that would do fine, Sandra. On my desk in the morning?'

'Yes, Angela. . . .'

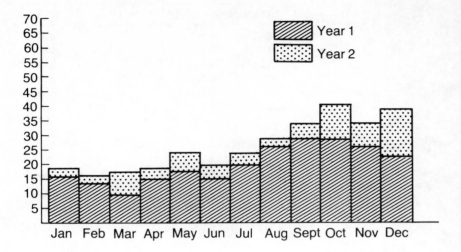

**Figure 22.1   Gross sales figures for Honeypot Biscuits' products for
first two calendar years**

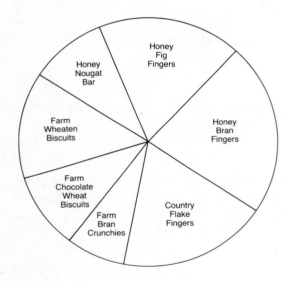

**Figure 22.2   Individual brand sales
of Honeypot Biscuits' products
for last sales year**

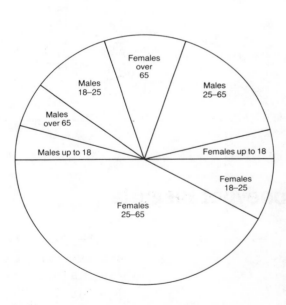

**Figure 22.3   Results of sample survey of
purchasers of Honeypot Biscuits' products
for last sales year**

Assignment

Under the headings which appear for each graph/chart,
summarize what appears to be the important information or
trends that are suggested. A paragraph (or two at the most)
should be sufficient to interpret the main points of information.

23 The writing of narrative and resolution minutes

Meetings

Practically all meetings have one factor in common: they aim to draw on the knowledge and opinions of a number of people in order to arrive at a democratically agreed decision or plan of action. A meeting may be regular or irregular. It may call itself a committee, a study group, a steering committee or an advisory body. Whatever its name or particular aim, the principle behind a meeting is based on the belief that, generally speaking, a number of minds working together should be able to arrive at a more satisfactory conclusion than a single mind.

There are other advantages to meetings, apart from the theoretical excellence of decisions reached. The feeling generated within an organization that the decision-making process involves employees at different levels is distinctly beneficial and breaks down the invisible barrier between management and workers. If decisions reached are not quite so successful as the group envisaged then the blame is shared and the difficulties of management are more widely appreciated.

Committees are usually organized in some sort of structure. A typical committee will include a chairperson, secretary and perhaps a treasurer and publicity officer. There will, of course, be ordinary committee members.

Roles of committee members

1 *Chairperson*   This important post (often elected) involves the following:
    (a) guiding and running actual meetings in such a way that members are allowed to have their say;
    (b) maintaining adherence to procedures expected at meetings;
    (c) ensuring that the agenda is drawn up beforehand and adhered to in the meeting itself;
    (d) acting as arbiter in discussion and, if necessary, having the casting vote.
2 *Treasurer*   Some committees will not have need for a treasurer but where this post exists the following are the usual functions and responsibilities:
    (a) recording over a period any financial transactions for which the group or organization is responsible;
    (b) submitting reports to the committee (at each meeting or annually) and keeping balance sheets available for inspection and approval;
    (c) advising the committee on financial matters generally.

3   *Committee member*   Not everybody serving on a committee will have an official position. The majority of people will be ordinary committee members and have the following important responsibilities:

(a) participating fully in meetings by offering opinions and information relating to matters on the agenda;

(b) feeding back to the people he or she represents the work the committee is doing;

(c) performing work delegated by the committee in its long-term decision-making role.

4   *Secretary*   The secretary has a demanding schedule of responsibility. The secretary's duties will include:

(a) advertising the arrangements for place, time and agenda of forthcoming meetings;

(b) carrying out administrative duties delegated by the committee and/or chairperson;

(c) assisting the chairperson as required;

(d) recording the minutes of meetings and having them ready for approval at the next meeting of the committee.

It is the recording of minutes that is most often associated with the work of a committee secretary. It is highly unlikely that a new or junior employee would be expected to undertake the arduous and responsible task of minuting a meeting. What is more likely is that junior employees find themselves in a position where it is necessary to read, consult or interpret the minutes of a committee meeting. In this case an understanding of how and why minutes are written will be of great importance.

Minutes

The minutes are simply an official record of what took place at a meeting in a condensed or summarized form. They contain the answers to the questions . . . Where? When? Who? What?

Where/When?

The minutes will show at an early stage in the recording of events *where* and *when* the meeting took place, eg:

> Minutes of the meeting of the Safety Committee of Norchester College held on 16 July 19-- in the Business Studies' staffroom at the Helmshore site at 4.15 pm.

Who?

If the committee or meeting is reasonably small, those present will be listed by name and those who could not attend and who sent their apologies will also be listed, eg:

> *Present*: Simon Andrews, Charlotte Mason, Gregory Hinds, Alice Nuttal, Alan Hunt, Martha Dickenson (chairperson).
> *Apologies for absence*: Clive Tweedale, Robert Preston.

If the meeting is a large one, such as a staff or union meeting, it may be that numbers will be sufficient, eg:

> Seventy-eight members were present with Martha Dickenson as chairperson.

What?

The minutes should be a record of the main strands of discussion as well as a statement of proposals made and the result of any voting that took place. The minutes will also conclude with a reference to the time, date and place of the next meeting if this has been arranged.

Having attempted a general definition of what minutes are, it should be said that the definition is rather simplistic as there are really two kinds of minutes: *narrative* minutes and *resolution* minutes.

Narrative minutes

This style of minuting is quite frequently used by small and informal societies or clubs is a way of narrating the 'story' of what took place at a meeting.

A person reading such minutes would get a good, overall picture of the background and discussion leading up to the final decisions made. Most people at the meeting who contributed to the discussion will have a version of their remarks recorded.

Advantages of narrative minutes

1 Some members will be attracted to attend the meeting in the knowledge that a summary of their remarks will appear in the final minutes.
2 Those members who are not in agreement with the democratically reached decisions will be on record as having 'known better' if the decisions turn out to have been the wrong ones in later experience.
3 A thorough picture of the whole meeting will be presented.

Disadvantages of narrative minutes

1 Narrative minutes can be very lengthy as virtually everything said at the meeting has to be summarized.
2 Some members will disagree with the minuting secretary's summary of what they actually said at the meeting.
3 Difficulties can arise with the reported speech that it is necessary for the secretary to use in writing the minutes. This might especially apply to selection of the correct verb tense when writing a record of what will be read in the future. It is also important to bear time intervals in mind, eg:
> 'The chairperson asked that a letter expressing the committee's condolences be sent tomorrow.'

If the above is read at a later date it will not make much sense and it should have been expressed as:
> 'The chairperson asked that a letter expressing the committee's condolences be sent the following day.'

In the world of business it is most likely that an alternative to narrative minutes will be employed. Instead of the full 'story' of the meeting with all the discussion and background information included, only the decisions reached are recorded. These are resolution minutes.

Resolution minutes

This style of minuting only records the proposals (or *motions* as they are termed in committee jargon), together with the names of *proposer* and *seconder* (the person and his/her supporter who put a motion to the committee). The results of any voting on the motions is also often recorded. Once a motion has been voted on and accepted then it becomes a *resolution*. The committee is then bound to run its affairs in accordance with the resolution. For example, if the motion: THAT THE OPENING HOURS OF THE COMPANY'S LONDON STORES BE EXTENDED BY AN EXTRA HOUR IN THE EVENING is proposed by Mr James, seconded by Mrs Harvey and accepted as a resolution after voting, then it is necessary that the opening hours be extended by the agreed hour as a part of company policy.

The disadvantages of resolution minutes

1   They are sometimes so brief that it is difficult on later reading to realize the lengthy discussion and debate that occurred before the motion was finally passed or defeated.
2   No record is kept of possibly useful counter-argument.

The advantages of resolution minutes

1   They are free from distracting and irrelevant material.
2   They are an objective and unprejudiced record of a meeting.
3   They are brief and to the point.
4   Since these minutes draw attention, by definition, to the resolutions passed, they are a clear and unambiguous record of what has become company policy and practice.

Presentation of minutes

The minutes that you might need to consult in the world of work are most likely to be resolution minutes. The example that follows, in order to illustrate a businesslike layout for the presentation of minutes is a set of resolution minutes.

```
                    TOWNLEY THEATRE COOPERATIVE

Minutes of the policy steering committee meeting held on Wednesday
6 October 19-- in Rehearsal Room 2 at 3.30 pm.

PRESENT:  Charlotte Langdon (chairperson), Helen Pickup, Tim Catterall,
          Will Smythe, Tony Clark, Tracy Astin.

APOLOGIES FOR ABSENCE:  Clyde Sullivan.

1  Minutes of the previous meeting
   Resolved: THAT THE MINUTES OF THE MEETING ON 7 SEPTEMBER 19--,
   PREVIOUSLY CIRCULATED, BE ACCEPTED AND SIGNED AS AN ACCURATE RECORD.
```

2 Matters arising
A report from the local fire officer following an inspection prior to
the renewal of the performance licence was still awaited.

3 Letter to Mr Sullivan
Resolved: THAT A LETTER EXPRESSING THE STEERING COMMITTEE'S REGRET AT
MR SULLIVAN'S CONTINUED ILL HEALTH BE SENT BY THE SECRETARY WITH THE
COMMITTEE'S BEST WISHES FOR A SPEEDY RECOVERY.

4 Sponsorship of future productions
Resolved: THAT THE SECRETARY, WITH THE HELP OF INTERESTED MEMBERS,
DRAW UP A LIST OF LOCAL COMPANIES WHICH MIGHT BE PROFITABLY
APPROACHED WITH A VIEW TO PROVIDING SPONSORSHIP OF FUTURE
PRODUCTIONS.

5 Any other business
Production clashes. The meeting was informed of the intention of the
Townley Women's Theatre Guild to perform Macbeth a week prior to the
Townley Theatre Cooperative's similar production.
Resolved: THAT THE SECRETARY CONTACT THE TOWNLEY WOMEN'S THEATRE
GUILD IMMEDIATELY IN ORDER TO INITIATE DISCUSSION ON FUTURE LIAISON
IN PRE-PRODUCTION PLANNING.

6 Date of next meeting
There being no other business, the next meeting of the policy
steering committee was provisionally arranged for Friday 25 October
in Rehearsal Room 2 at 4.00 pm.
The meeting ended at 4.45 pm.

Signed:
(Chairperson)

Date:

You will see, on studying the minutes, that the business and
discussion that took place between six people for one and a
quarter hours has been summarized in about a page. Resolution
minutes allow this brevity and contain, for the record, the main
decisions of the meeting.

In fact there may have been heated and detailed discussion at
the meeting but the objective style adopted keeps personalities in
the background and facts and decisions in the foreground.

Note

1 The numbering of items in the order in which they are allowed
discussion by the chairperson.
2 The numbering begins with the resolution for acceptance of
the previous meeting's minutes.
3 The numbering ends with the arrangements for the time and
place of the next meeting.
4 The use of subheadings to draw the reader's attention to the
topics and areas of debate.
5 The way in which a friendly agreement to send best wishes to
a sick colleague is put into resolution form so that the record
shows the committee's sympathy.

24 Ongoing case studies

Honeypot Biscuits

Sandra examined the notes she had made when taking the minutes of a discussion chaired by Mrs Jarvis and attended by a number of section heads. It had been a particularly lively meeting and she had the task of converting her narrative notes into resolution minutes for the official record.

Here is an extract from Sandra's notes which records the discussion which took place on a particular issue half-way through the meeting.

---

5 <u>New packaging for export lines</u>

Mrs Jarvis opened the discussion on this topic by announcing that the first firm order had been received for a number of Honeypot Biscuits' products from Mr Pisi and his chain of retail outlets in Zambia. Mrs Cooper, production supervisor, expressed her pleasure at the order but enquired why new packaging would be required as the current packaging seemed very attractive.

Mr Daldry of the sales section agreed that the current pack, with its attractive design was a considerable factor in achieving a good market share.

Mrs Jarvis pointed out that since the decision had been made to air-freight the order direct to Lusaka, in order to avoid delays in shipping and rail transport, it would be necessary to reduce the weight of the current cardboard pack.

Mr Botham of Finance and Accounts suggested that if there was to be a new pack it would have to be no more expensive than the present one as the air-freight costs were already cutting into profit margins.

Mr Daldry suggested that shrink film wrapping of the product would cut down on weight, be cheaper and allow a new logo or design suitable for the African market to be incorporated. Mrs Jarvis suggested that if a wrapper could be designed which incorporated the Zambian national colours of red, green and black the problem might be solved.

Mr Daldry added that this kind of packaging might also avoid problems of shelf life in the humid Zambian climate.

It was unanimously agreed that Mrs Cooper should approach the usual supplier of packaging to discuss costs and design of colour printed shrink film wrapping.

Sandra breathed a sigh of relief. Although the discussion had been somewhat wordy, the fact that resolution minutes were required meant that this particular section of the minutes was recorded as follows:

---

5 <u>Discussion and proposal for new packaging of export lines</u>

Resolved: THAT THE PRODUCTION SUPERVISOR DISCUSS WITH MAPLIN PACKAGING THE DESIGN AND COST OF A THREE-COLOUR DESIGN ON SHRINK FILM WRAPPING SUITABLE FOR AIR-FREIGHT TRANSPORTATION.

Sandy Bay Leisure Services

Tracy was less than pleased. Tracy was really rather angry. It had taken her quite some time to write up her notes at the end of a rather rowdy meeting of the Parks and Public Gardens Sub-Committee. She was convinced that Mr Bickerstaffe had asked for narrative minutes. When he breezed into the office and announced that the minutes were fine but he had only wanted resolution minutes, Tracy found great difficulty in keeping a polite smile on her face.

<u>SANDY BAY LEISURE SERVICES DEPARTMENT</u>

Minutes of the meeting of the Parks and Public Gardens Sub-Committee held on Friday 3 November in the Conference Room of the Town Hall at 10.00 am.

<u>MINUTES</u>

<u>PRESENT</u>: A Bickerstaffe (chairperson), A Carter, D Moon, S B Downey, K Wintersgill, D Fletcher.

<u>APOLOGIES FOR ABSENCE</u>: H Slinger

1 <u>Minutes of the previous meeting</u>
Mr Wintersgill drew members' attention to the apparent typing error in Item 5, Employment under MSC schemes. The reference to 'one-year schemes' should read 'two-year schemes' as was plain from the resolution that followed. Members were asked to correct their copies accordingly. The minutes were then approved and signed by the chairman as a true record.

2 Matters arising

The secretary reported that as a result of the committee's request, she had written to the local training officer of the Manpower Services Commission to invite him to discuss current problems being experienced by employees on MSC training schemes. A reply had not yet been received.

3 Replacement of railings along northern boundary of Cliffside Park.

The head gardener reported that estimates had been received from three suppliers for replacement of the Victorian railings on the northern edge of Cliffside Park. The cheapest of these estimates was £6450.00. The maintenance officer suggested that unless the new railings were galvanized and rust treated the annual painting cost would be in the region of £750.00 per year at current costs. There was some dismay at these financial estimates. The head gardener suggested that the planting of quick growing evergreen hedging would be a long-term solution and would cost approximately £1250.00. The maintenance officer wondered what the clipping and trimming costs might be. It was estimated that such a hedge would only need attention every three years and that this could be undertaken as one of the intermittent duties of the park's staff. It was unanimously agreed that the head gardener undertake a programme of hedging along the northern boundary of Cliffside Park as an alternative to replacing the metal railings.

4 Vandalism to benches on the western side of the Promenade Gardens

It was reported that in the current financial year four wood and metal benches had been thrown into the sea by vandals. In addition to structural damage there had been an outbreak of spray can graffiti on three more benches. This painted graffiti had cost about £75.00 to clean off and repaint. In a desperate attempt to combat damage to benches an attempt had been made to drill and bolt them to the terracing so that they could not be moved. Regretfully the previous night had seen one bench uprooted and thrown into a flower bed. The cost of replanting the affected bed was approximately £37.00. The chief gardener suggested that the problem was becoming worse and that with increased costs the committee might consider removing all benches from the Promenade Gardens. The chairman suggested that the area was popular with senior citizens and that to remove any opportunity for them to sit and enjoy the gardens was a retrograde step.

The maintenance officer suggested that if the benches were to be retained it would require an increase in the maintenance budget to cover the costs of repair.

The finance officer enquired whether the committee had considered replacing the old fashioned wood and metal benches with cast concrete structures. These were virtually maintenance free and could not be moved to cause damage to themselves or flower beds.

It was felt by the chief gardener that the appearance of modern, cast concrete benches would be entirely out of keeping with the Victorian atmosphere of the Promenade Gardens.

The chairman suggested that the maintenance officer look at ways of ensuring the currently used benches could be anchored more securely to the terracing. The chief gardener enquired whether easily cleaned 'graffiti-proof' paint was available to protect the benches. The committee agreed that the maintenance officer look into these two possibilities.

5 Any other business

The chief gardener enquired whether any news had been received from the Department of the Environment as to EEC regulations relating to safety equipment being available in the area of ponds and lakes in municipal areas. The secretary confirmed that a letter had been sent to the headquarters in Bristol but a reply was still awaited. The chairman declared that since the incident involving three children who had fallen into the boating lake was still a cause for concern, another letter should be sent to the Department of the Environment. The committee all agreed that this was a matter of some urgency.

6 Date of next meeting

There being no other business, the next meeting of the sub-committee was provisionally arranged for Friday 17 November in the Conference Hall of the Town Hall at 11.00 am.

The meeting ended at 11.55 am.

Date: Signed:

                                (Chairperson)

Assignment

As accurately as possible, using a typewriter if possible, rewrite the above narrative minutes as resolution minutes.

25 Drawing up an agenda and designing a proposal

The agenda

(A)
(B)
(C)

LITTLE HAZELDENE FILM SOCIETY

THE NEXT COMMITTEE MEETING WILL TAKE PLACE ON FRIDAY 15 AUGUST
19-- IN HAZELDENE TECHNICAL COLLEGE DRAMA STUDIO (ROOM 109) AT
6.15 pm.

(D)
(E)

AGENDA

(F)

(1) Apologies for absence.

(2) Minutes of last meeting.

(G)

(3) Matters arising from the minutes.

(4) Correspondence - suitability of films for family
     membership in June's programme.

(H)

(5) Proposal to increase membership fee:
     THAT THE ANNUAL MEMBERSHIP FEE BE INCREASED BY £5.50 TO
     COVER THE INCREASED COSTS OF FILM RENTAL.
     Proposer: James Henderson
     Seconder: Tracy Slade

(I)

(6) Problems with condition of chairs used at film viewings.

(J)

(7) Any other business.

(K)

(8) Date of next meeting.

(The letters (A) to (K) at the side of the agenda are referred to later.)
This agenda of the Little Hazeldene Film Society is presented in the format that is commonly accepted by a business organization as appropriate for the structure of a meeting.

Planning the agenda

Some time well in advance of the proposed meeting, the chairperson and secretary will meet to decide on the contents of the agenda. The accepted conventions of an agenda's presentation mean that the actual layout on the page is already decided. (Chapter 23 has already dealt with the agenda from the point of view of the *minutes* of a meeting.)

Although decisions have to be made concerning (B) and (C) – the time and place of meeting – it is not until the items after *Matters arising* that decisions have to be made with regard to content and the order in which items will be dealt with at the meeting.

In the example we are looking at, items (4), (5) and (6) have *not* been put in this order in an arbitrary fashion. The chairperson, in consultation with the committee secretary, has decided that the correspondence should be dealt with immediately after matters arising from the minutes. The correspondence in this case is a letter from a member who regularly writes to complain of the unsuitability of the films chosen for viewing by the film society. Since the committee has twice previously discussed this person's objections to the film programmes and has twice rejected the arguments, the chairperson wishes to deal quickly with this item. The reason for placing the correspondence item so early in the meeting is that the opening items (1), (2) and (3) are usually passed over very quickly and without much discussion. By placing the correspondence item so close to these introductory items the secretary and chairperson hope that the discussion will continue to be brief and not waste too much of the meeting's time.

Item (5), which is a proposal made prior to the meeting, is expected to generate a lot of discussion. The proposed increase in annual membership fee will affect all those who are already in the Film Society as well as having a possible effect on the recruitment of new members. This important item is not placed later in the agenda as it is possible that towards the end of the meeting members may start to grow weary of discussion and press for a vote on the issue before all aspects of the issue have been thoroughly discussed.

Item (6), which deals with the condition of the chairs used for seating at film viewings, has come up for consideration before. It is a long-standing problem and will not be resolved at this one meeting. The chairperson has indicated to the committee secretary that placing this item towards the end of the agenda will mean that if the discussion goes on for too long it will be possible to cut it short because of lack of time.

Items (7) and (8) are always placed at this end of the agenda for obvious reasons.

The agenda and the committee secretary's role

(A) Either headed paper is used for the agenda or the secretary types the organization's title very clearly in underlined capitals.

(B) The date (and possibly time) of the meeting will probably have been decided at the end of the previous meeting, although it is sometimes left to the chairperson's discretion to work out an appropriate day.

(C) The arrangements for the room will have to be made by the secretary and a firm booking made if the venue is hired from another institution.

(D) Apologies for absence will have been received by the secretary (or the chairperson and passed on to the secretary) prior to the meeting. These could have been written apologies or sometimes a message is passed on by telephone. During the actual meeting the secretary will take down the names of those whose apologies are sent via members who are present.

(E) The minutes of the last meeting will have been written up shortly after the previous meeting. Copies of these can either be sent out to members with the agenda before the next meeting or else be available for reading and approval on the day of the meeting. The chairperson will have been shown the minutes previously.

(F) The secretary is responsible for acting on any directions given by members at the previous meeting and reporting back to the meeting any results that may be available. For example, at a previous meeting the membership may have instructed that an approach be made to a number of hotels to obtain quotations for the cost of a celebration dinner for the membership. In this case the secretary should present to the meeting, under 'matters arising', the results of approaches made to local hotels or restaurants.

(G) A copy of any correspondence that has been received and which the chairperson believes should be brought to the attention of the meeting should be available at the meeting.

(H) If a proposal has been received by the secretary or chairperson since the previous meeting, this must be put in the agenda in appropriate form. If the proposal has not been put in 'proper' proposal form, it is up to the secretary, in consultation with the chairperson, to put it into the appropriate wording. This new form of the original suggestion must be checked with those from whom it had originated to ensure that it is what they want the meeting to discuss. For example, James Henderson and Tracy Slade had approached the secretary with the suggestion: 'We think that with rising prices charged by so many film rental companies we could do with putting up the membership by five or six pounds.'

It was then up to the secretary to put it into the more formal proposal form and then check with Henderson and Slade that this was what they wished the meeting to discuss and vote upon.

(I) This item could be suggested by anyone in the membership who asked that some discussion take place. There is no proposal but it is possible that a proposal might arise out of the discussion that takes place at the actual meeting.

(J) Any items suggested for discussion which come to the secretary or chairperson after the agenda has been drawn up can be included under 'Any other business'. At the chairperson's discretion, items for 'AOB' can be accepted at the commencement of the meeting itself. It is up to the chairperson how many items are allowed in this category at any one meeting.

(K) The secretary should have a diary with details of any other commitments listed so that the meeting can be made aware of any 'impossible' dates when the date of the next meeting is being discussed.

The wording of a proposal

Something that an individual member (and a seconder) wish to have discussed and voted on at a meeting has to be put to the meeting in the form of a proposal. By custom a particular form of wording has come to be accepted as almost universal practice. This wording is primarily concerned with the introductory words of the resolution. For example, if someone's intention is to stop people smoking in the works' canteen by asking for a discussion and vote on the issue at a staff committee meeting, he or she will be asked by the chairperson or secretary to put the idea into proposal form. This might be:

'THAT DUE TO HEALTH HAZARDS CAUSED BY SECONDARY INHALATION, SMOKING SHOULD NOT BE PERMITTED IN ANY PART OF THE WORKS' CANTEEN.'

Proposals that are put formally, in the hope that they will become resolutions, always start with 'THAT' – followed by the details of the proposal, put as briefly as possible.

26 Ongoing case studies

Honeypot biscuits

Mrs Jarvis was discussing with Sandra the forthcoming meeting of the Forward Planning Committee. The next meeting was due to take place on Friday 18 December but the committee secretary was away from work with a virus infection.

'I'm sorry Sandra but I've just got to get the agenda out to the committee members. Fortunately they're all in the works so we won't have the delay of posting.'

'How soon does the agenda have to be got out, Angela?'

'I normally like the committee to have a week to think about some of the ideas and proposals.'

'But it's the 10th today and the committee secretary's still away on sick leave isn't he?'

'Exactly, Sandra,' said Mrs Jarvis, meaningfully.

'I see,' replied Sandra, beginning to realize what was coming.

'You must have covered this kind of thing at college, Sandra – minuting procedures, agendas, that sort of thing?'

'Well . . . yes, but . . .'

'Splendid, Sandra. I've got a couple of points that I'd like to put to the meeting for discussion and I've received a formal proposal from Mrs Cooper on behalf of the Staff Association. I've had verbal apologies from Karen Warner and Trevor Lee who have to be at a meeting with the Trading Standards Officer on the 18th.'

'Have you got details of the time and place for the meeting?'

'Yes, I've written it all down for you. There's also a list of the committee members so that you can get the final agenda sent out to the appropriate departments. I think everything you need is on these sheets of paper. I'm sorry they're all in a bit of a mess but I'm sure you'll make sense of them.'

'Very well, Angela.'

'Oh, Sandra. I've put an asterisk by the point I want discussing in some depth. It's really quite important, so make sure it gets placed suitably in the order of business will you?'

'I'll do my best.'

Here are the notes in the same random order that Mrs Jarvis presented them to Sandra Kong. (If Sandra had been the normal committee secretary there would have been much more detailed discussion with the chairperson but in this case Sandra was on her own.)

Forward Planning Committee meeting scheduled for Friday 18 December.
Given the absence of Karen Warner and Trevor Lee, I think there will be room enough to use my office for the meeting.
(Check that there are enough chairs please Sandra.)

Forward Planning Committee
Chairperson - Angela Jarvis
Secretary - Mary Hughes
Members - Charles Jarvis
Gill Taylor
Arthur Owen
Karen Warner
Trevor Lee
Catherine Cooper
Alan Botham

INTERNAL OFFICE MEMORANDUM

TO Mrs. Jarvis

FROM The Staff Association

REF ....

DATE ....

SUBJECT .....Canteen facilities.................................

For a number of months now we have discussed the facilities for
refreshments. While welcoming the recent improvements, we would
like the Forward Planning Committee to discuss the following
proposal: THAT A CATERING MANAGER BE APPOINTED AND FULL CANTEEN
FACILITIES BE PROVIDED FOR BOTH SHIFTS.

Proposer: Mark Riley

Seconder: Celia Martin

Sandra
These are items for
discussion that I want
to raise at the Forward
Planning Committee meeting
on 18 December.
* (a) With the success of
shrink wrapping for exports
to Zambia and the economies
experienced, I would like
the committee's views on
a shift to this type of
wrapping for all our
products.
(b) A fresh look at our
logo and the use of it on
our packaging and company
vehicles and delivery vans.

Assignment

1 Using the layout for an agenda that has been shown in Chapter 25, pull together the various strands of information and requests that Mrs Jarvis left with Sandra into a neatly presented agenda. (Remember the asterisked item for discussion.)

2 List the departments within the Honeypot Biscuits organization that need to be sent a copy of the agenda in order for it to reach the appropriate committee members.

Comment

If your typing is up to it, try typing the finished agenda. In the world of work a handwritten agenda would be totally unacceptable, no matter how neat your handwriting.

When making the list of departments, remember that there have been two apologies for absence.

Sandy Bay Leisure Services

The Centenary Gala Concert had been a disaster. The weather, a strike by newspaper printers and the fact that the master of ceremonies and compere of the concert was taken into hospital on the morning of the concert combined to make the event a social and financial flop of alarming proportions. The Finance Officer, the town council and the rate-payers of Sandy Bay were protesting with some fury at the event which had been, in every sense of the word, a 'washout'.

'The Finance Officer was on the phone again, Arthur.'

'If he rings again say that I'm out, Tracy. This nightmare never seems to end.'

'Well they can't blame you for the weather, can they? You couldn't forecast that a Force 10 gale was going to blow all day.'

'And you wouldn't think that I'd be blamed for the printers' strike that stopped all the newspapers that carried our advertisements being published!'

'But we'll get the advertising fees back won't we?'

'Yes, but that's nothing compared to the loss we made on the concert and fire-work display, not to mention the champagne supper.'

'The evening made a loss did it?'

'You could say that, Tracy! The Finance Officer estimates that we'll be about £4500 down after all the contractor's bills are settled.'

'That much?'

'At least. Look, I'm calling an emergency committee meeting of the Centenary Committee. We've just got to adjust the programme for the rest of the celebrations. I've already had a formal proposal from the Finance Officer and I've got a couple of items for discussion suggested by members in the Library Arts Centre and the Parks and Gardens section.'

'And you need an agenda quickly?'

'I need it by this afternoon and in the hands of committee members by tomorrow morning. We'll have the meeting in the Conference Room at 9.30 in the morning, the day after tomorrow. That will be Wednesday 19 December, I've phoned around and, barring sickness, everybody will be OK for Wednesday, so there are no apologies for absence at the moment.

'You'll find all the details you need in my "out tray". Get it drawn up, photocopied and in the internal mail system by this evening please. I'm off to talk to the local newspaper editor about some cheaper rates for any later advertising.'

'Shall I show it to you before sending the agenda out, Mr Bickerstaffe?'

'Ordinarily yes, but time is all important and I'm not sure what time I'll be back, Tracy. Oh, by the way, put the Finance Officer's proposal last thing on the agenda please. I think the items from the Arts Centre might influence the committee's thinking by the end of the meeting.'

Here are the items that Tracy found in Mr Bickerstaffe's 'out tray' and which she had to put together to form an agenda for the meeting of the Centenary Committee.

1

Proposal from the Sandy Bay Municipal Finance Office

We would like to place the following proposal on the agenda of the next meeting of the Centenary Committee.

THAT ALL FUTURE EVENTS TO WHICH THE LEISURE SERVICES DEPT IS COMMITTED IN THE PERIOD OF THE CENTENARY CELEBRATIONS BE CANCELLED EXCEPT WHERE BREAKING OF CONTRACTS ALREADY ENTERED INTO WOULD CAUSE FURTHER FINANCIAL LOSS.

Proposer: Stephen Willoughby

Seconder: David Bamber

2

Item for discussion at the next meeting of the Centenary Committee (sender - Acting Head of Library Arts Centre).

After lengthy negotiations, the Library Arts Centre has just been informed that the European Economic Community's Cultural Fund has just released a sum of £2750 to be used at the discretion of the municipality to stimulate cultural events in the region.

Can a proportion of these funds be used to support the Centenary Celebrations?

3

Item for discussion at next meeting of the Centenary Committee (sender - Chief Gardener of Parks and Gardens section).

I have been approached by Lord Worth of Worth Hall to discuss with him assistance from the municipality in his plans to open his gardens to the general public.

He requires advice on the labelling of shrubs and trees as well as estimates of maintenance costs. In private conversation he has indicated that in return for advice and guidance in the preparation of his gardens for visits by the public, as well as some assistance with maintenance, he would be prepared to enter into a 50-50 division of gate receipts for a period of twelve months initially.

Lord Worth's collection of sub-tropical plants as well as alpines is nationally famous and would attract a large number of visitors from outside the region.

4

```
MEMBERSHIP OF CENTENARY COMMITTEE

CHAIRPERSON - Head of Leisure Services

SECRETARY - Tracy Donaldson

MEMBERS - Councillor Andrews
          Alan Spence
          Percy Boulsworth
          Agnes Duerden
          Bernard Hughes
          James Doherty
          Simon Taylor
```

Assignment

1   From the information relevant to the meeting that is contained in the conversation between Mr Bickerstaffe and Tracy as well as in the notes 1 to 4 above, draw up an agenda for the 'emergency' meeting of the Centenary Committee.

2   Checking back on the details of the suggestions given for formulating a proposal, turn the item for discussion in 3 into a formal proposal on behalf of the Parks and Gardens section. Assume that the proposer is James Doherty and the seconder Alan Spence.

27 The telex – its language and layout

What is telex?

The telex system allows you to send a letter by using the telephone. You sit at your telex keyboard, which is very similar to that of a typewriter, and type out a message to someone in another part of the country or another part of the world. If you ignore the electronic details involved, a telex machine and its printer are a combination of a typewriter and a telephone.

If your job involved use of a telex machine and teleprinter, there is no doubt that you would receive specialized training on the operation of such a machine. This section will attempt to give you some initial guidance on the principles behind the system, the operation and design of telex messages and their interpretation.

The advantages of telex

Speed

A telex message can be transmitted swiftly. A trained operator in an office may well be able to transmit at a rate between 50 and 60 words a minute. The advantages over a letter sent by first class or air mail are obvious, especially when one bears in mind that the telex message is printed out for its receiver instantaneously.

Accuracy

When a message is transmitted to a foreign country in which the language is different, the written printout of a telex message can be translated with care. This avoids the problems of misunderstandings which may arise from telephone conversations in which different languages are being spoken by the parties concerned.

Product

A telex printer presents both sender and recipient of a message with a record of the communication. At the same time as the operator of the telex is typing out the communication, the printout is being received at the other end of the line of communication. Up to 10 copies can be produced by modern telex teleprinters, which is useful for a group of decision makers communicating by telex.

Time flexibility

Business hours are virtually 24 hours a day when telex equipment is installed. Urgent messages can be sent to an office long after staff have gone home and a printout will be waiting for action or reply as soon as the receiving office is staffed again. International business communication is made easier as time differences in other parts of the world are not so awkward when messages can be received or transmitted during the standard working hours of either party.

Economy

Telex equipment is not cheap, either to buy or rent, but operation can be cheaper than a telephone when the machine is operated by a skilled secretary. The added advantages of printouts make a telex machine a useful piece of office equipment for businesses of a certain type and scale.

Comparison of communication by telex and by letter

The letter

1 Letter is dictated.
2 Letter is typed up from the dictation pad.
3 Letter is checked and then signed.
4 Letter is put in internal mail system.
5 Letter is stamped or machine-franked.
6 Letter is posted.
7 Letter is sorted at post office.
8 Letter is transported by road and rail (and air, if overseas).
9 Letter is received and read by recipient.

If there is a reply to be made, the whole process is gone through again. By the time the reply is in the hands of the original sender of the letter, a series of *18 processes* will have been gone through and there will have been a time lag of days (at least).

The telex

1 Message is dictated.
2 Message is transmitted.
3 Message is received and automatically printed out.
4 A reply is dictated.
5 The reply is received and automatically printed out.

The whole process of transmission and reply has taken only *five stages* and the time lag is virtually nil. The only time involved is dependent on the speed of the operator and the decision time needed to formulate a reply.

The telex keyboard

The keyboard is very similar to that of a standard typewriter. With the exception of some additional keys and the absence of lower case letters (all letters printed are CAPITALS) a typist would feel reasonably at home with the layout.

The main additional keys are:

1 FIGS   The depression of the key with this marking opens up the system and allows the next two keys to be used.
2 WHO or WHO ARE YOU   The depression of this key allows identification of the other telex operator. This is a check against sending a message to the wrong recipient. (The equivalent of dialling a wrong number on a telephone.)
3 BELL   This key causes a warning to be signalled on the machine of both the sender and the receiver. The warning indicates that transmission is about to take place.
4 FEED or LINE FEED   This is the equivalent of the 'shift arm' on a manual typewriter and moves the display (if a visual display unit is used) or the paper (if a printout is used) up a space to allow the next line of the message to be typed in.
5 LTRS or LETTER   This key allows the rest of the keyboard to be used to print out the message, as on a standard typewriter.

In addition to these keys there will be a dial as on a telephone or a push-button dialling panel (as on many modern phones). This is used to dial the individual telex number of the organization to which the message is to be sent. The telex numbers are looked up in a telex directory in the same way as a telephone directory would be used.

How to make a telex call

As has been said already, you will have received special training before you use a telex machine to transmit actual messages. This training might take place in your office and be undertaken by an operator who has already been trained or the training might be given by the Telecom service itself. What follows is a simplified guide to what you might expect to find when training actually starts.

1 Press dial button.
2 Dial the required telex number.
3 Check that the transmission or receiving light has come on. (It is usually green.)
4 Check that the other telex machine operator or the machine itself (if operating outside business hours or across time zones) has sent back the correct 'answerback code'. (This avoids a 'wrong number'.)
5 Type out message.
6 Teleprinter or visual diplay unit (or both) show transmitter and receiver of message what is being written.

At any stage in the transmission of the message, operation of the BELL key by transmitter or receiver causes an alarm signal to ring on both machines which draws attention to a difficult or ambiguous part of the message. The transmitter can adjust the message to clarify the meaning by pressing the SPACE BAR and retyping the offending section of the message.

Modern telex machines are much more sophisticated than the earlier versions, having *text editing facilities* (to allow the operator to ensure that the message is correct before it is actually sent), *automatic redialling* (if the line is initially engaged), *multiple despatch* (of the same telex to, for example, all branches or subsidiaries of a company), *cost calculation and logging* and *prioritization* (so that all urgent telexes are sent, automatically, before less urgent ones). Because of this, and of better telecommunication links between different countries, the possibility of error is greatly reduced. However you are still likely to encounter codes which were developed to assist earlier operators in speedy questioning and response; some of the more usual ones are shown here.

ABS   – Operator absent or office closed.
CFM   – Confirm please.
COL   – Repeat please. (This would be used by a receiving
          operator to check on difficult words or vital figures.)
CRV   – Are you receiving well?
DF   – You are in correct contact with desired operator.
EEE   – Error.
NOM   – Waiting for transmission.
NR   – Please indicate your number.
OCC   – Telex number engaged.
OK   – Do you agree? (or Agreed)
R   – Received.
RAP   – You will be called back.
RPT   – Repeat or Repeat please.
SVP   – Please.
TAX   – What is the charge? *or* The charge is . . .
WRU   – Who am I speaking to?
+   – Message ends.
++   – There will be no further message.

Example of telex message

```
845866 POLTOR-G
55123 AGHOLD-RS

25/11/87    10.00    K3412


ATTN MR J ROBERTS


WE MUST DRAW YOUR ATTENTION TO CHANGE IN REQUIRED
SPECIFICATION INCLUDED IN OUR ORDER NO 10/177.

PLS ACKNOWLEDGE AT EARLIEST OPPORTUNITY.


REGARDS


55123 AGHOLD-RS
845866 POLTOR-G
```

Comment

1 The first line of the telex displays the telex number (845866), answerback code (POLTOR) and country identification (G) of the organization to which the telex has been sent. 'G' is the international designation for Great Britain.
2 The second line is, similarly, the number and code of the sender of the telex. RS is the international code for Singapore.
3 The date, time and, optionally, an internal reference are shown.
4 The receiving answerback code is repeated at the end of the message to confirm that the receiving machine is still 'on line' and has received the message; the sender's code then confirms that transmission is over.

English in use

Spelling – Formation of negatives by addition of prefixes

This section will demonstrate the dangers of misspelling when adding a prefix to a word.

1 *UN* is the most common prefix added to a word to form its opposite or negative form. Even this prefix can cause problems unless used carefully. There is little problem when converting words like:

FORTUNATE – UNFORTUNATE   EXCITING – UNEXCITING
HAPPY – UNHAPPY   WORTHY – UNWORTHY
PLEASANT – UNPLEASANT

Problems can arise, however, when the word to which the prefix *UN* is added starts with the letter *N*. The following words often cause casual spellers some problems.

NATURAL   NOTABLE
NECESSARY   NAVIGABLE

There is a temptation simply to put a *U* in front of the word since there is already an *N* in place. Such spellings would be incorrect. So long as you remember that the prefix you should add is *UN* then there should be no trouble. (Always assuming that you know how to spell the base word!)

The correct spelling of the 'awkward' words just listed would be:

UNNATURAL
UNNECESSARY
UNNOTABLE
UNNAVIGABLE

2   *DIS* is another prefix used to form the negative of a word which can cause problems. Although there is little problem with words such as:

PLACE – DISPLACE
ALLOW – DISALLOW
HONOUR – DISHONOUR
INFECT – DISINFECT
OBEDIENT – DISOBEDIENT

There can be problems when you forget that the prefix you are using is *DIS*. This is very likely when the word to which you are adding the prefix already begins with *S*.

Words like DISSATISFY and DISSIMILAR are sometimes spelt without the *double S* that adding this prefix demands.

Other *DIS* words that cause people problems for some reason are:

DISAPPEAR
DISAPPOINT
DISAPPROVE
DISAGREE

3   *IL, IM, IN* and *IR* are other prefixes which mean *NOT*.

As long as you remember the spelling of the word to which you are adding the prefix, you should not go far wrong. You must also remember that the full prefix must still be added to base words which begin with the same letter as the last letter of the prefix, eg:

ILLEGAL	IMPATIENT	INDECENT	IRRELEVANT
ILLEGIBLE	IMMATURE	INNUMERABLE	IRREGULAR

Exercise

Use appropriate prefixes in the spaces found in the following sentences. You can check the accuracy of your answers by referring to a good dictionary.

1   The cake was . . .perfect because of a lack of sugar.
2   The crashed car was . . .movable.
3   The bargains in the sale were quite . . .expensive.
4   I am . . .satisfied with your work.
5   Your handwriting is careless and . . .legible.
6   His attendance at classes is rather . . .regular.
7   The accident was most . . .fortunate.
8   The calculation was . . .accurate
9   Although they are brothers, their appearance is quite . . .similar.
10   It is . . .necessary to put your hand up.

28 Ongoing case studies

Honeypot Biscuits

```
238722 HONEY-G
42763 PIRLUK-ZM

05/01/88    09.45

FOR ATTENTION MRS A JARVIS

WE MUST REPORT THAT WE HAVE ONLY RECEIVED HALF OF OUR
ORDER 12/738/11.

PLS CONFIRM WHETHER ORDER IS SENT IN TWO PARTS.

THANKS,

PIRI


42763 PIRLUK-ZM
238722 HONEY-G
```

The above telex has been received by Honeypot Biscuits. It is from Mr Piri's business headquarters in Lusaka, Zambia. It refers to the recent air-freight shipment of Honeypot Biscuits' products.

Exercise 1

Referring to the coded abbreviations and comments on layout given earlier in Chapter 27, write a short paragraph in which the message and details are expressed in your own words for reporting to Mrs Jarvis.

A telephone call to Trans Continental Air Freight, who were responsible for carrying the order to Zambia, has confirmed that the order was dispatched in two parts. The second flight is due to deliver the remainder of the order at approximately 16.00 hours Zambian time on 7.1.88.

Exercise 2

Using the examples of telex layouts given elsewhere in this chapter and in Chapter 27, design a telex reply to Mr Piri's enquiry concerning the missing part of his order. You should use a typewriter, if possible, and remember that on a real telex keyboard only capital letters are available.

Comment

It may be helpful to your design and laying out of the telex reply if you work with someone else in order to reach joint decisions and to check that you have used the telex format correctly.

Sandy Bay Leisure Services

The following telex has been received by Alicia Mitchell at the Town Hall central office and the printout copy passed on to Mr Bickerstaffe for his urgent attention.

```
     266422  SBAY-G
     825524  JTA-G

     07/01/88    09.30    1-82


     URGENT

     ATTENTION HEAD OF LEISURE SERVICES DEPARTMENT

     WE MUST INFORM YOU AS A MATTER OF SOME URGENCY THAT
     THIS AGENCY NO LONGER REPRESENTS TONY TREMOLO.

     ANY CONTRACT BETWEEN MR TREMOLO AND YOURSELVES IS NO
     LONGER A RESPONSIBILITY OF THIS AGENCY.


     JILLY THOMPSON AGENCY


     825524  JTA-G
     266422  SBAY-G
```

Tony Tremelo had been contracted, via his agent Jilly Thompson, to star in the next season's summer show. Mr Bickerstaffe was somewhat alarmed at this development as top class entertainers need to be booked well in advance. A replacement would be difficult to find at this stage. The doubt concerning the contract with Tony Tremelo had to be resolved quickly.

In order to discover which theatrical agent now represented Tony Tremelo there were two choices open to Mr Bickerstaffe.

1 He could contact the Jilly Thompson Agency to see if it had details of the new agent.
2 He could telex Equity (the performers' union) to see if it had a record of the new agent.

Exercise

With the help of a telex directory (if necessary) compose a telex to either the Jilly Thompson Agency or Equity in London, enquiring about the new agency representing Tony Tremelo.

29 More work on pie charts, bar graphs and composite bar graphs

Reminder of limitations

It was suggested in Chapter 21 that pie charts and bar graphs are useful for giving a quick, visual impression of statistics and the comparison of statistics. It must be emphasized, however, that they are of limited use when very precise details are required. It is, of course, possible to be accurate when designing and interpreting such charts and graphs but fine precision is difficult to achieve. Having said that, there is no doubt that such displays are very useful 'tools', within their limitations.

Although there is some limitation to the absolute precision of the statistics that can be shown (without resorting to graph paper as in a conventional graph) a most useful comparison can be made.

Horizontal bar graph

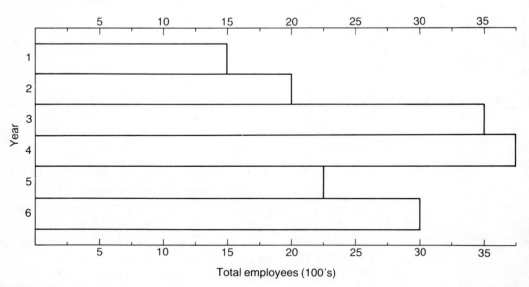

Figure 29.1 Horizontal bar graph

The bar graph (Figure 29.1) is no different in essence to the vertical bar graphs illustrated in Chapter 21. For some people, turning the bars into a horizontal plane allows the changes to be more quickly appreciated and the readings, which are available for checking at the top *and* bottom of the chart, to be more easily checked.

Exercise

From the bar graph (Figure 29.1), check the answers to the following:

1 Which year saw the company employing the highest number of staff?
2 How many staff were employed in the year of highest employment?
3 Which year saw the company employing the second lowest number of staff?
4 How many staff were employed in the above year?
5 What is the difference in the number of staff employed in the fourth year of production and the first year of production?

Composite horizontal bar graph

If we wish to show a breakdown of the figures for staff employed in terms of male/female/full time/part time, we can represent the details as shown in Figure 29.2.

Figure 29.2   Composite horizontal bar graph

In order to interpret the details in any one year represented in the composite bar graph (Figure 29.2) we must first examine the key. If we take the *first* year as an example, we learn:

1 That the total workforce numbered 1500.
2 That the part-time staff totalled 750.
3 That the female staff totalled 250.
4 That the male staff totalled 500.

Exercise

From the same composite bar chart (Figure 29.2), check the answers to the following:

1 In which year did the company employ the largest number of female staff?
2 In which year did the company employ the smallest number of female staff?
3 In which year did the company employ the smallest number of part-time staff?
4 In which year did the company employ the largest number of male staff?
5 In which year were the numbers of part-time, female and male staff most evenly balanced?

Another way of presenting the staffing situation over a number of years as well as the composition of the staff is shown in Figure 29.3.

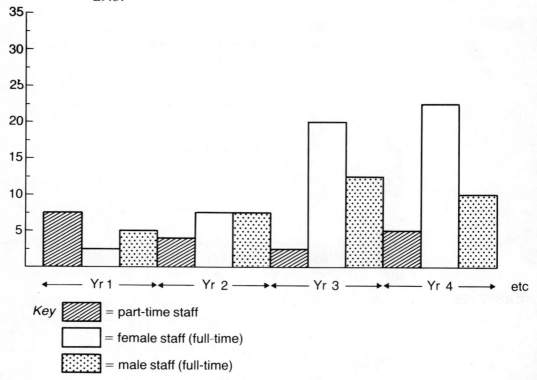

Figure 29.3   **Vertical bar chart**

Pie chart

A pie chart is *not* capable of showing comparisons between years without presenting a pie chart for each individual year. A pie chart, as we know by now, *is* useful for showing, visually, the composition of a whole.

The staff composition of the company that has been used as the source of statistics for the previous graphs would be shown as in Figure 29.4 for the first year of production.

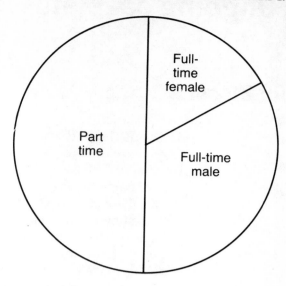

Figure 29.4   Pie chart of staff composition

You may recall from Chapter 21 the formula used to work out the space of the 360° circle occupied by the different slices of the pie. The known total is always 100 per cent of the circle and the different sections which make up the total are represented as percentage portions of the whole. If we take the last example we will see that:

1   The whole pie represents a workforce of 1500.
2   The part-time staff (750) are 50 per cent of the total and, therefore, their slice will be exactly half of the pie (180°).
3   The full-time male staff (500) are one-third of the total and, therefore, their slice will occupy 120° of the pie.
4   The full-time female staff (250) are one-sixth of the total and, therefore, their slice will occupy 60° of the pie.

Exercise

1   Make a pie chart to represent the composition of the workforce for the above company in the sixth year of production.
2   Make a pie chart of which the whole represents the full-time female workforce in the six years of production. Each slice should represent the size of the full-time female staff in each year of production.

Comment

The figures on which to base your calculatons for 'slice' sizes may be gained from any of the relevant bar graphs previously shown.

30 Ongoing case studies

Honeypot Biscuits

The annual report was imminent and Mrs Jarvis wished to emphasize the progress made by Honeypot Biscuits over the last four years. She was particularly keen to draw attention to the improvement in employment opportunities she was bringing to the local area by the steadily increasing size of the workforce as well as showing the rise in output and turnover.

'Sandra, I've been looking at this section on statistics in the appendix to the annual report and I'm not very happy with it,' said Mrs Jarvis with a concerned expression.

'Have I made a mistake typing up the figures?' enquired Sandra.

'No, nothing like that. The figures are completely accurate. It's just that they don't tell the story of our development unless the reader is prepared to go through the figures very carefully.'

'Would you think that something more visual would help?'

'Exactly what I was thinking, Sandra. We've got a few more days before distribution of the report. Do you think you could illustrate the figures for *output*, *turnover* and *employment* by graphs and pie charts?'

'Very well, Angela.'

Here are the figures from the report's appendix that Sandra used as the basis for the visual display requested by Mrs Jarvis.

Comparison of gross output over a four-year production period
(Measurement in hundredweight units)
YEAR ONE   : 1700 units
YEAR TWO   : 3500 units
YEAR THREE: 14 000 units
YEAR FOUR : 19 000 units (estimated figure based on 11 months' production)

Comparison of gross turnover in a four-year trading period
YEAR ONE   : £68 550
YEAR TWO   : £220 500
YEAR THREE: £890 750
YEAR FOUR : £1 320 550 (estimated figure based on orders received in current financial year)

Comparison of staffing figures over a four-year period
YEAR ONE   : 3 female, 2 male
YEAR TWO   : 6 female, 3 male
YEAR THREE: 11 female, 6 male
YEAR FOUR : 12 female, 15 male

Assignment

Checking the advice and examples given in Chapters 21, 22 and 29, on the design and interpretation of charts, graphs and diagrams, make an attempt at the following:

1 Present the figures for gross output over the four-year production period as *either* a suitably labelled pie chart *or* a vertical or horizontal bar chart.
2 Present the figures for gross turnover in a four-year sales period as a composite bar graph (vertical or horizontal).
3 Using the figures for male and female employment figures over the four-year period, design *either* four suitably labelled pie charts *or* a vertical comparative bar graph to illustrate the employment pattern.

Sandy Bay Leisure Services

The following sets of figures represent the expenditure and the receipts from the Centenary Concert, together with the advanced booking receipts for events planned for later in the celebrations. The figures have been supplied by the Finance Officer for Mr Bickerstaffe's consideration. Tracy is required to present the figures to the Planning Committee for discussion.

Expenditure (up to 31.1.19--)

Media advertising	£1175.00
Overtime payments to staff	£520.00
Fee for firework contractor	£2200.00
Fees for performers at Centenary Concert	£3750.00
Catering costs (incl. champagne supper)	£1265.0
Printing costs for programmes, leaflets, tickets (incl. all planned celebration events)	£1190.00

Receipts (up to 31.1.19--)

Advanced ticket sales (Centenary Concert only)	£3700.00
Ticket sales on night of Centenary Concert	£250.00
Refreshment sales at concert	£90.50
Advanced ticket sales for champagne supper	£350.00
Sale of souvenir programmes	£55.00
Advanced booking sales for later Centenary Celebration events	£4550.50

'Tracy, I've been looking over the figures and one thing is pretty clear.'

'What's that, Arthur?'

'We can't allow the rest of the events in the Centenary Celebrations to be cancelled.'

'The advanced booking sales for the later events certainly do look quite healthy.'

'Exactly. If we cancel the forthcoming events then that £4550.50 will have to be given back to the customers and we really will be in a financial mess.'

'How do you think the Planning Committee will react?'

'I think I'll be able to talk them round. What I believe to be very important is to present these figures in as persuasive a way as possible, Tracy.'

'What would you like then?'

Mr Bickerstaffe requested Tracy to present *two* comparative bar charts. The first was to compare the figures for expenditure and receipts using the *total* figures presented by the Finance Officer. The second was to present the totals for expenditure (since none of this money could be reclaimed) against the totals for receipts *minus* the £4550.50 for sales of tickets for future events. The latter comparative bar graph would show the financial effect of cancelling the celebrations.

Exercise

Design:

1 A comparative bar chart that presents the totals of expenditure and receipts for comparison based on the totals of the figures presented.
2 A comparative bar chart that presents the totals for expenditure and receipts but does *not* include the advance booking sales for later events (£4550.50).

Comment

You should not find your mathematical ability unduly stretched as nothing more advanced than careful addition and subtraction is required for the exercise. You should shade or colour your bars distinctly. If you were to use red to represent expenditure and blue to represent receipts, you should find that the second comparative bar chart has considerably less blue than the first chart.

31 Some techniques of persuasive writing

Both inside and outside the world of work we find ourselves in situations where we need to write persuasively. The situations may range from the very personal (a love letter) to the essentially practical (a letter of application for a job), from the relatively mundane (a request for information) to the vital (a company report persuading shareholders to support a radical change in policy). What these different situations have in common is a need, on the part of the writer, to exploit the appropriate techniques of writing and choice of language in order to achieve a persuasive effect.

A number of factors should be borne in mind when writing to persuade, whatever the particular situation.

Sentence length

You may have noticed that the final sentence of the opening paragraph of this chapter was not particularly easy to read. I hope it was not incomprehensible. Although the sentence is grammatical and reasonably well structured, it is too long. Its 34 words are in excess of the length that many experts believe is the limit beyond which the average reader finds irritation. There is obviously no hard and fast rule which can be automatically applied, but 20–25 words is commonly taken as a sensible limit.

Sentences should be of a length that a reasonably intelligent reader can hold in mind easily. It is very annoying to have to go back to the beginning to pick up the thread of an argument that has got lost in the sheer length of the sentence.

This does *not* mean that all sentences should be short.It does *not* mean that all sentences should be in the 20–25 word range. The ideal paragraph or piece of writing will contain a variety of sentence lengths. The length of sentence will be chosen to fit the subject matter of the sentence. The commonsense point I wish to make is that you are hardly likely to persuade someone if your sentences confuse or irritate because of their length. For example, disregarding other factors, such as choice of language, which of the following do you find more acceptable as a reader?

1 I would be obliged if you would arrange to meet me this afternoon in my office to discuss the problems that seem to be arising with regard to the punctuality of your arrival at work over the last few weeks.

2 Please come to my office this afternoon. I would like to discuss your recent unpunctuality.

Register

A factor that must be considered when choosing language to persuade is register. There are three elements that, in combination, make up what we mean by this term:

1 *Field*   This refers to the subject matter under discussion. We would clearly use a different type of sentence and vocabulary depending on whether we were discussing political theory or the quality of ice-cream.
2 *Tenor*   This refers to the level of formality required by the situation and by those communicating. An audience with the pope or a prime minister would be conducted at a different langauge level from a chat with a mate over a coffee.
3 *Mode*   This refers to the method of communication or quite simply whether we are speaking or writing.

A combination of these three elements should always be borne in mind when deciding on the register of our remarks. The person that you are trying to persuade with your language has certain *expectations*. He or she has certain status (in a work sense) which is above, below or equal to yours.

It is *not* a matter of being excessively humble if you are trying to persuade the managing director or excessively colloquial if you are addressing the new junior assistant. Both the 'boss' and the 'junior' are more likely to respond positively if the language you choose is appropriate to the circumstances and shows suitable respect for their power to do something for you. For example, which of the following do you feel more appropriate in the circumstances?

To the 'boss'

1 I would really be most obliged if you could see your way to granting me a day off work due to the fact that I am moving house next week.
2 I am moving house next week. Would it be possible for me to have the day off?

To the 'junior'

1 I need File 190B and I need it now. Get it to my desk immediately.
2 I urgently need File 109B. Please could you bring it as soon as possible?

Euphemism

A dictionary defines 'euphemism' as 'a way by which an unpleasant or offensive thing is described in milder terms'. A typical example is when the fact of *death* is replaced by euphemistic terms such as: *passing away, meeting one's Maker, the eternal sleep, no longer with us*, etc.

Sometimes the use of euphemism is either silly or deceptive. Advertisers and salespersons often indulge in highly imaginative use of euphemism. A house described by the person selling it as 'in original condition' may, in fact, be 'in desperate need of repair'. Chapter 3 illustrated this abuse of language when discussing synonyms and antonyms. In this case we are considering the euphemism as a useful tool in persuading an individual or a group that a situation or action is not so unpleasant as it might have initially been considered. For example:

There will be an opportunity to earn considerable overtime payments next week. (Euphemism)

You will have to work late all next week. (Fact)

Or

I'm sure you will appreciate the benefits of plenary staff development courses. (Euphemism)

You must attend a series of staff training courses. (Fact)

Choice of language

Apart from the particular factors of sentence length, register and use of euphemism, there is the general question of selecting the right word or phrase in order to persuade. Chapter 3 reminded you of the synonyms that are usually available to achieve accuracy and appropriateness of expression. The English language is so rich in vocabulary, and shades of meaning, that more often than not there is an alternative to the word or phrase that first comes to mind.

It is impossible to be specific since the situations and choices available are virtually infinite. All that can be said is that whenever you are writing with the intention to persuade (and you are probably writing with this intention more often than you would think) you should check that there is not a synonym or alternative phrase that would do the job better. Tact and diplomacy go hand in hand with persuasive writing. For example, to which of the following instructions would you more willingly respond?

1   Workers must not turn up for work sloppily dressed.
2   Staff should ensure that their dress is not casual but appropriate to the work place.

Exercise

By alterations in either length, register, euphemism or choice of synonyms, adjust the following sentences so that they are more likely to persuade.

1   Your scruffiness is intolerable and you had better smarten up or you'll get your cards.

2 You'll have to stay late tonight as I'm behind in my correspondence.

3 I want a complete breakdown of the staff attendance record on my desk by 3.00 pm prompt.

4 I'm feeling knackered with this wretched cold and I could really do with the afternoon off. What do you say?

5 Last year's trading figures were disastrous and if we don't get the workers to accept some sackings or a cut in the wage packet the company will go bust.

32 Ongoing case studies

Honeypot Biscuits

There had been a number of problems with quality control at Honeypot Biscuits. The new shrink film packaging certainly ensured the freshness of the product but offered little protection from damage while in transit to the wholesalers and retailers. There had been an additional problem caused by over-baking which made several of the batches over a three-day production period extremely brittle and rather unpleasant to the taste.

'Sandra, I've decided that a circular letter must go out to all our customers. These packaging and quality control problems are going to lose us business if we're not careful.'

'I thought that we were going back to the old style of packaging, Angela?'

'For the home market that's true. The problem of quality control should be overcome by the new appointment of a production line inspector, but the retailers who have been having complaints from the public don't know that. I've a pile of letters on my desk, all complaining of problems with damaged biscuits or over-baking.'

'Are you going to send a letter to each of the complainants?'

'I'm sending a letter out to everyone who had a delivery from the production of those disastrous three days last month. There may be some customers who can't be bothered writing to complain. They'll just order from a different manufacturer next time.'

'That could be a lot of letters, Angela.'

'According to the office we could be talking about 150 different customers. That's why I want a circular letter drafting.'

'Sounds like it will have to be a pretty diplomatic piece of writing.'

'That's why I've done a sort of outline. I'll leave the actual writing to you. I've just jotted down the main points that I want included. Could you manage to draft a version by this afternoon, Sandra?'

'I'll certainly try.'

Here is the outline for a circular letter that Mrs Jarvis left with Sandra.

Dear Customer,

Para (1) Apologize for impersonal nature of circular letter. Introduce subject of letter, ie damage caused by new packing methods and faulty batches over a three-day period causing over-baking.

Para (2) Assure customer of immediate return to traditional packaging methods. Refer to appointment of production line inspector to ensure no possibility of future faulty products.

Para (3) Credit to be given on next order from customer for all goods returned as complaints.

Para (4) Assure of continued standards of quality associated with our products in future. Look forward to continuation of valued business relationship.

Assignment

Draft the circular letter that Sandra should complete for Mrs Jarvis. You should act on any relevant advice you have noted in Chapters 3, 7, 13, and 31.

You should use the paragraph order of Mrs Jarvis's outline and ensure that you include all the issues within the paragraphs as suggested. Concentrate on using language as persuasively as you feel appropriate in the circumstances.

Sandy Bay Leisure Services

Dear ....

The entertainments' programme for next year is to be expanded to include International artists in the field of comedy, dance, music as well as arts and crafts exhibitions throughout the season.

Cutbacks in government support of leisure provision and a desire by Sandy Bay Borough council to cut down on rate increases means that the proposed programme is in danger.

We should welcome your financial support of next year's programme in the form of sponsorship. Such sponsorship could be for individual events or take the form of general sponsorship for the season's programme.

The benefit of such sponsorship would be to the community as a whole and your business in the form of publicity. All sponsors will be acknowledged in press publicity as well as on posters and programmes.

We would welcome the opportunity to discuss your possible involvement in this exciting new development.

Yours faithfully,

'Tracy, I'm not very happy with this circular letter I've just drafted.'

'Do you want me to check it for spelling and layout, Arthur?'

'It's not the spelling or layout that I'm bothered about, thank you very much, Tracy. It just doesn't sound sufficiently persuasive.'

'Would you like me to have a go at rephrasing it?'

'Would you? I'd be very grateful, Tracy. It's vital that we get local sponsorship for next year's programme of leisure events. The Finance Officer has made it very clear that our budget will not be increased for next year. We were lucky not to have the rest of the Centenary Celebrations cancelled.'

'I'll try to make it a little more persuasive then.'

'Thanks Tracy. Don't turn it into a begging letter. I'll need to have a look at what you manage by tomorrow morning. We can go through it together then.'

Assignment

Using whatever means you believe will be successful, redraft Mr Bickerstaffe's circular letter, proposing business sponsorship of the leisure programme, into a more persuasive form.

Your letter should contain most of the information that Mr Bickerstaffe's draft contains but make sponsorship sound more attractive to the potential sponsor. The letter should not be longer than one side of A4 paper, typed with double spacing.

33 The use of information sources

As you will have realized from previous chapters, the potential sources from which information may be gathered are many and varied. From posters to encyclopaedias, from timetables to computer memory banks, we live in a world that is increasingly filled with information. The more information that is available, the more difficult it can be to isolate and extract the particular information that we require in some specific circumstance.

If we take, as an example, a person going on a journey which involves travel to, and accommodation at, the place of destination, the following questions will need to be answered:

1 How far away is the destination?
2 How long would it take and how much would it cost to travel by car, rail or air?
3 What type of accommodation is available at the destination and what range of prices will this entail?
4 What factors would it be useful to know about the destination?
5 What might the cost of travel insurance be?

Some of the above questions are very specific and can be discovered relatively easily.

The answer to the *first question* will be a geographical fact and can be checked by the use of an *atlas* or *map*.

The answers to the *second question* would involve more extensive research. The time-consuming research could most easily be delegated by a phone call or visit to a *travel agent*. One could presumably work out an approximation of the time and cost of travel by car for oneself (assuming that the distance, fuel consumption and cost of fuel is known). The cost and length of the journey by rail and especially air are best left to a travel agent. The variety of airlines and seat costs can be very great and a computer-equipped, modern travel agency would be able to work out the required details very quickly.

The answers to the *third question* would be available by reference to one of the following: a motoring organization *handbook*, a tourist board *brochure*, an accommodation *list* from the information office of the destination concerned.

The answers to the *fourth question* (which is a very general one) might be found from a wide variety of sources. Some of the sources used in researching question 3 might provide the desired information. In addition one might find useful information in a town *guide*, an *encyclopaedia* or even a geography *textbook*.

The answer to *question 5* (which is very specific) could be found by consulting the *leaflets* issued by various insurance companies which list the rates for a variety of periods and destinations for which insurance of health or baggage is required. An *insurance broker* would have all the information required (as well as a travel agent).

Reference books as sources

The reference section of a college or municipal library should include examples of the following books.

1 *Keesing's Contemporary Archives* – a record of international events culled from news agencies and the press.
2 *Chambers Technical Dictionary* – a guide that explains technical terms from a wide variety of industries.
3 *The Statistical Yearbook (UNO)* – a record of statistics concerning agriculture, population, industry, education, etc, for most of the nations of the world.
4 *Roget's Thesaurus of English Words and Phrases* – a guide to words and their synonyms.
5 *Pears Cyclopaedia* – a general reference work.
6 *Motoring 'Which' Guide* – a consumer guide to cars, involving extensive testing and suggestions of value for money.
7 *Plain Guide to the Law* – a simplified guide to the law and legal practice.
8 *Fowler's Modern English Usage* – a guide to accepted style in English grammar.
9 *Writers' and Artists' Year Book* – listings of publishers, journals, agents, magazines, advice on copyright law, income tax, etc.
10 *The Guinness Book of Records* – a listing of world records in a wide variety of events.
11 *The Oxford Dictionary of English Place Names* – an explanation of the origins of village, town and city names.
12 *The Everyman Dictionary of Quotations* – a listing of famous quotations, their source and original dates of usage.
13 *Who's Who* – a regularly updated dictionary of biography of notable men and women in public life.

Exercise 1

Go to the reference section of a school, college or town library and see how quickly you can discover the answers to the following questions. It would be a sensible idea to make a brief note by each question of the information source that you believe might be useful. In this way you will be able to know how many questions you are trying to answer from a particular reference source and time will be saved.

1 What were the dates of the Boer War?
2 What is the insurance group rating of a Vauxhall Cavalier 1600?
3 What is a reed valve?
4 What was the name of the President of Argentina during the Falklands conflict with Britain?
5 Who said, 'I have nothing to declare but my genius'?
6 What is the origin of the town name Winchester?
7 Should one say or write 'compared with' or 'compared to'?
8 Which publisher produces *Woman's Own*?

9   Where did Vanessa Redgrave train for her career in Drama?
10   Which country won most silver medals in the last Olympic Games?
11   If your neighbour's apple tree overhangs your garden, are you allowed to help yourself to the apples on your side of the fence?
12   What is the overall fuel consumption of a Volkswagen GTI?
13   How many counties are there in Wales?
14   What are five other words for 'drunk'?
15   Which country has exported most coffee in the last ten years?
16   What precisely is the law of trespass?
17   Who said, 'Power corrupts, absolute power tends to corrupt absolutely'?
18   What is a 'double overhead camshaft'?
19   Is there any copyright on the title of a book?
20   What is the longest river in Scotland?

Comment 1

If you are using contents pages and indexes properly, you should be able to find most of the answers within 40 minutes.

In the earlier part of this chapter an example was given of the questions a person might wish to find answers to before going on a journey. In the following exercise you should use your home town as the base and imagine you are planning a business trip which requires you to be at a conference for a Saturday and Sunday from 10.00 am on Saturday morning to 4.00 pm on Sunday afternoon.

Exercise 2

1   What is the distance from your home town to your capital city?
2   Estimate the cost of travelling to the conference by car, by rail and by air. (You should use whatever information sources are available.)
3   What is the range of costs of bed and breakfast accommodation in the capital? (The highest and lowest costs will be adequate.)
4   What is the address of the Canadian High Commission, the YMCA, a swimming baths, a Ford agency?
5   What is the cost of insuring yourself against accident and luggage loss for the duration of the journey from home and back to home after the conference?

Comment 2

You should use the most convenient sources of information for this exercise. These might include: libraries, agencies, people, books, guides, etc.

English in use

Homophones and other confusing words

In Chapter 13 we looked at the problems caused by words which have a similar or identical sound but different spellings and meanings.

Here are some more homophone pairs that you may find trouble with in your writing.

Exercise 1

Without the use of a dictionary (at first anyway), try to use each word in an appropriate sentence. When you have completed as many sentences as you can manage, use a dictionary to check your results (and also to help you complete those you had to miss out).

ASCENT	BEAR	CEILING	COUNCIL
ASSENT	BARE	SEALING	COUNSEL
DRAFT	FARE	GRATE	HOLD
DRAUGHT	FAIR	GREAT	HOLED
LEASED	LIGHTENING	MIND	NEW
LEAST	LIGHTNING	MINED	KNEW
PRINCIPAL	RAIN	SHORE	STATIONARY
PRINCIPLE	REIGN	SURE	STATIONERY
THERE	WEATHER	WEAR	WAIT
THEIR	WHETHER	WHERE	WEIGHT

In addition to the above homophones there are other words that may cause you problems. You could get caught out by either the spelling or interpretation of some of the following often confused words.

INGENIOUS	PROCEED	PRACTICAL
INGENUOUS	PROCEDURE	PRACTICABLE
INDELIBLE	ELIGIBLE	DECENT
INEDIBLE	ILLEGIBLE	DESCENT
ELEVATING	HIRE	LIBEL
ENERVATING	HIGHER	SLANDER
EXCISE	WONDER	ALTERNATE
EXERCISE	WANDER	ALTERNATIVE

The above words can create difficulties because of their similarity of appearance, sound or usage. In some cases the difficulty is caused by habitual carelessness rather than inherent difficulties in the words themselves.

Exercise 2

Without the help of a dictionary, use each of the above words in a sentence that clearly shows its proper usage. When you have completed as many as you can, refer to the dictionary to check your use of the word and to help you to complete the exercise.

34 Ongoing case studies

Honeypot Biscuits

Mrs Jarvis has been invited to visit a new customer for Honeypot Biscuits' products in Canada. The customer wishes to discuss the possibility of a new range of products being supplied that would be suitable for the Canadian market. Since the market is potentially of great importance, Mrs Jarvis has decided to fly out to Canada. She intends to visit a manufacturer of hard grain wheat flour in Alberta while she is there to see whether a contract for regular supply can be arranged.

'Sandra, I'll need you to fix me up with a flight to Canada for Monday next. I'm visiting Steven Cellik in Toronto to discuss the possibility of contracting for a new range of biscuits. I also want to visit Jill Casey of Alberta Millers in Calgary. I'll need a flight from Manchester to Toronto on Monday morning and then a flight from Toronto to Calgary on the following Thursday morning. I've got to be back in Toronto by Friday evening to finish my discussions with Steven Cellik. Finally, I want a flight from Toronto that will get me back to Manchester by Sunday afternoon at the latest.'

'That doesn't sound too difficult, Angela. I'll get on to it right away.'

'That's not quite everything, Sandra. I'll need a hotel booking in Toronto for the nights that I will be there and a hotel for the night in Calgary. I'd also like you to find out the addresses of the Chambers of Commerce in Toronto and Calgary as well as the names of the three top selling biscuit manufacturers in Canada.'

'Is that all?'

'That's it thanks. If you could jot down the relevant details for me I'll see if there's anything we've missed. Oh, if you could also check whether I need a visa for a short business trip to Canada, I'd be grateful.'

'I'll do my best, Angela.'

ITINERARY FOR MRS JARVIS'S BUSINESS TRIP TO TORONTO AND CALGARY

FLIGHTS (a) 'Wardair' flight 112C departing Manchester Airport 09.30
            hours, Monday 3 March. (Check in one hour before
            departure.) Flight arrives Toronto 11.30 hours local time.

        (b) 'Air Canada' flight 105 departing Toronto International
            Airport 08.15 hours, Thursday 6 March. (Check in 30 minutes
            before departure.) Flight arrives Calgary 11.25 hours local
            time.

        (c) 'Air Canada' flight 601 departing Calgary Airport 13.45
            hours Friday 7 March. (Check in 30 minutes before
            departure.) Flight arrives Toronto 16.50 hours local time.

        (d) 'Wardair' flight 115B departing Toronto International
            Airport 05.30 hours Sunday 9 March. (Check in 45 minutes
            before departure.) Flight arrives Manchester 17.15 hours
            GMT.

HOTEL ACCOMMODATION
TORONTO   Maltravers Tower Hotel, 1255 Yonge Street, Toronto, Ontario.
               Single room for Monday night to Wednesday night (3-5 March).
               Single room for Friday and Saturday nights (7-8 March).

CALGARY   Mountain View Hotel, 69 Baxter Avenue, Calgary, Alberta.
               Single room for Thursday night (6 March).

CHAMBERS OF COMMERCE
TORONTO   Toronto Chamber of Commerce,
               1156 Queen Elizabeth Street
               TORONTO
               Ontario   (Telephone 458 - 6655)

CALGARY   Alberta Chamber of Commerce,
               120 Trail Street
               CALGARY
               Alberta   (Telephone 246 - 5050)

CANADIAN BISCUIT MANUFACTURERS
(1) Craig Thomas Bakers Ltd (Hamilton, Ontario)
(2) Maple Products (Vancouver, British Columbia)
(3) Spencer Products (Toronto, Ontario)
(In order of volume sales for last year)

VISA
A visa is not required for a visit lasting less than 10 days.

Sandy Bay Leisure Services

'I suppose you've heard about this invitation to visit our opposite numbers in the Sports and Recreation Department of our twin town, Tracy?'

'La Rochelle? Well, yes I did hear a rumour to that effect, Arthur.'

'It's more than a rumour; it's a fact. We've had an invitation to travel over with half a dozen representatives to look at their way of running things in La Rochelle. The invitation's come at a very bad time, I must say.'

'How's that?'

'From the point of view of diplomacy we've got to go but financially this is a very bad time to be spending funds on a trip to France, even if it is only a three-day visit.'

'Problems with the Finance Officer again?'

'Exactly.'

'Would you like me to do an estimated costing of a three-day visit to La Rochelle for six representatives?'

'I'd be very grateful, Tracy. Our meals and accommodation in La Rochelle will be at the expense of their Sports and Recreations Department. I need a breakdown of transportation costs for six people travelling by coach or rail or air to La Rochelle. We'll also have to be responsible for meals on the journey there and back. The normal expenses payable to municipal officials for such costs on council business are £7.50 per 12 hours and then £2.50 each three-hour period beyond 12 hours until the destination is reached.'

'I think I'll be able to work out a figure from that, Arthur.'

Assignment

Using the travel expenses allowed by Sandy Bay Council, and La Rochelle in south-west France as your destination, work out the cost of transporting six adults from *your* home town to La Rochelle and back. You should use whatever sources of information are available to you in order to find the cost of transporting the party by air, coach or rail (or possibly a combination of all three) to La Rochelle and back to base. You should also include in your calculations an estimate of the expenses payable to individuals on the outward and return journeys.

If you are *not* a resident of mainland Britain, use a similar number of travellers and the same expense rates but make the destination approximately 400 miles (or 650 kilometres) away from *your* home town.

35 Effective Use of the Telephone and a Message Pad

It is difficult to imagine how communication in business and private life was conducted before the telephone came into widespread use. It is a magnificent convenience and a terrible nuisance, by which is meant that, if used efficiently, the telephone can be a convenient tool to communication but if used carelessly it can cause confusion and delay.

Advantages of the telephone (if used efficiently)

1   The telephone can be a very quick and convenient means of giving and receiving information.
2   The telephone can be a relatively inexpensive means of communication if it is used sensibly and at the appropriate time of day.
3   The telephone enables follow-up to incoming enquiries to be made immediately. This could be advantageous to the business concerned.
4   The telephone allows clarification of any ambiguities at the time, which can lead to savings in time and money.

Disadvantages of the telephone (if used carelessly)

1   If significant details are not checked and written down at the time of the call, later confusion can result.
2   If used without care and at an inappropriate time of day, the telephone can be an expensive means of communication.
3   If key words, specifications or figures are not double-checked by caller and receiver, ambiguity can result with potentially expensive or wasteful consequences. Always check names, numbers and addresses.
4   If the tone of your voice is not friendly or courteous a poor impression may be received by a caller.

The cost of using the telephone

Apart from whatever rental and/or standing charges may apply to the possession of a phone, the cost of making any call is dependent on *when* you make a call and to *where* you make it.

When

At the time of writing, there are three charge rates in mainland UK for calls made in any 24-hour period.

1 *Cheap rate*   This relatively inexpensive rate is charged for calls made between 6.00 pm and 8.00 am from Monday and Friday inclusive. It is also charged for calls made at any time on Saturday and Sunday. (This cheap rate is not very useful for a majority of businesses as it falls outside standard working hours.)
2 *Standard rate*   This is the middle range rate charged for calls made between 8.00 am and 9.00 am as well as between 1.00 pm and 6.00 pm Mondays to Fridays.
3 *Peak rate*   This is the most expensive rate and is charged for calls made between 9.00 am and 1.00 pm Mondays to Fridays. This is the time when a majority of people wish to use the phone and, as the telephone service is a business, the charges reflect this demand.

Any company would obviously prefer calls to be made at the standard rather than the peak rate. Only if there is some urgency about the call should peak rate times be used to make contact.

Where?

At the time of writing there are three main categories of area or distance which affect the cost of a telephone call.

'B' rate

This is the most expensive type of call and applies to numbers dialled that are over 56 km (35 miles) from your base.

'A' rate

This charge is made for calls that are up to 56 km (35 miles) away but outside your immediate area.

'L' rate

This is the local area rate. Details of districts to which this rate applies can be found in your local telephone directory.

General points to note when making or receiving a call

1 When making or receiving a call you should ensure that you leave whichever hand you write with free to make notes of any relevant details that arise during the call.
2 Speak at a slower rate than your normal speaking voice and ensure that your pronunciation is very clear. Your speech will always appear quicker to a listener, especially a listener at the other end of a telephone.
3 Since the person to whom you are speaking cannot see your face or 'body language', ensure that you keep a courteous, friendly tone in your voice. Efficiency does not mean a lack of friendliness.
4 Always check before the conclusion of the call that your message has been understood and/or that you have fully understood any information given you.

Points to note when acting as *caller* on the phone

1   Make a note or list, if necessary, of points you wish to make during your call. By ticking off the points on the list as you make them it is possible to ensure that your call has achieved its desired purpose.

2   If you are phoning a company that is of a large scale and has a number of extensions, ask for the extension number as soon as you have got through to the main switchboard. If you do not know the extension number you need, ask for the person or department you require by name. (It is also a good idea to make a note of the extension number when you know it so that time can be saved if you have to contact the person or department again.)

3   Introduce yourself and the name of the company that you represent as soon as you have got through to the appropriate person or department.

4   As the caller, you should know when your call has come to an end. If your list is all ticked off and no other issues have arisen, it is up to you to bring the call to an end. Your thanks to the person who has taken your call and a polite 'Goodbye' are all that is required.

Points to note when acting as a *receiver* of a call on the phone

1   Always answer with a polite tone of voice by saying:
(a) Good morning/Good afternoon.
(b) Extension number (if this applies).
(c) Your name.

2   Make notes of the main points being made by the caller. It may be that a message is dictated to you. Ensure, by checking with the caller, that you have got the message accurately recorded.

3   Maintain contact with your caller by the occasional 'Yes' or repetition of a word or phrase. In this way the caller is ensured that you are paying attention and that the line has not gone dead.

4   If the call involves you taking a message on behalf of someone else in your organization, make sure that you have written up the message legibly, with date and time of call, for the intended recipient.

5   If you are asked for information which you do not have immediately to hand, you are faced with a choice.
(a) You may offer to ring back with the required information (if you believe your search will take some time).
(b) You may politely ask your caller to wait (if you believe the required information is close to hand or on file).

The design and use of a message pad

Most large organizations and businesses will provide printed or duplicated message pads on which details of calls may be recorded. If you find yourself in a place of work that does not provide such a facility, it would be a good idea to duplicate a number of your own, based on the following example.

TELEPHONE MESSAGE

FOR: DATE:

TIME:

CALLER:

CALLER'S No/Extension No:

CALLER'S ADDRESS

MESSAGE:

_____

MESSAGE TAKEN BY:

A telephone message pad is a much more orderly and efficient way of recording the essential details of calls that you receive either for yourself or on behalf of others. The pad should be filled in as your call proceeds. If you attempt to fill in the details once the call is over, you will be surprised how many details will have been forgotten.

Once it appears that the call is reaching a conclusion you should make a quick visual check that you have a record of all the essentials. If you find that there are breaks or blanks on your pad, you should politely ask the caller to give or repeat the missing details.

Dictating and receiving a message on the phone

The following 'script' serves as an example of how a conversation might be conducted on the telephone, during which a message has to be dictated for the urgent attention of a member of staff at the organization being called.

Receiver: Good afternoon. Extension 219. Sue Johnson speaking. May I help you?

Caller: Good afternoon. This is Charlotte Raynor of Micro Services. Could I speak to Mr Parker, please?

Receiver: I'm afraid that Mr Parker is out of the office at the moment. We are expecting him back by four-o'clock. May I take a message?

Caller: Yes, please. The message concerns Mr Parker's order, number 77051. (Pause)

Receiver: Order 77051. Yes?

Caller: There are three parts.

Receiver: Yes?

Caller: There has been an increase in the price of VDU Z105. (Pause)

Receiver: VDU Z105. Yes?

Caller: The price increase is £17.50. (Pause)

Receiver: £17.50.

Caller: Please advise if this increase is acceptable or whether you wish to re-order a cheaper model.

Receiver: Yes?

Caller: Secondly, the specification of the printout copier has been changed. Model PX200 is now compatible with word processor units produced in Europe and Japan. (Pause)

Receiver: Printout copier PZ200 . . . compatible . . . Europe and Japan. Yes?

Caller: Finally, the stencil correction fluid that was ordered is temporarily out of stock. We expect our suppliers to make a delivery to us before the weekend. (Pause)

Receiver: Yes?

Caller: Do you wish us to delay dispatch of complete order until the correction fluid is in stock or send the goods currently available? (Pause)

Receiver: I've got that, thank you.

Caller: If Mr Parker would like to ring me back with his decision later today, he can contact me on Highfield 67288, extension 215.

Receiver: Highfield 67288, extension 215. Thank you. I'll certainly give Mr Parker your message, Miss Raynor.

Caller: Thank you. Goodbye.

Receiver: Goodbye.

Points to note

1   The receiver has politely and quickly established her name and extension number.

2   The caller has politely identified herself, her organization and the name of the person to whom she wishes to speak.

3   The caller, on learning that Mr Parker is not available, has quickly gone on to state the topic of the message, ie 'order number 77051' and has warned the receiver that the message will be in three parts.

4   The caller details the three points in order, pausing to allow the receiver to note particular names/model numbers/prices.

5   The receiver keeps in contact with the caller by the use of a repeated 'Yes?' or repetition of a detail, eg 'Printout copier PX200 . . . compatible . . . Europe and Japan . . . Yes?'

6   The caller concludes by ensuring that her telephone and extension numbers are included in the message.

7   The receiver does not commit Mr Parker to returning the call but politely states that she will be sure to give him the message.

8   Both caller and receiver politely conclude the call when the business is over.

9   The call took place during the standard rate call charge.

10   The length of the call is approximately 1½ minutes.

The completed message form

At the conclusion of the above phone conversation the receiver's telephone message pad should appear as follows:

TELEPHONE MESSAGE

FOR: Mr Parker   DATE: 23 August 19..

TIME: 15.25

CALLER: Charlotte Raynor

CALLER'S No/Extension No: 77051 (ext 215)
CALLER'S ADDRESS Micro Services Ltd, High Street, Grange, West Yorkshire.

MESSAGE: Regarding Order no 77051
(a) VDU Z105 has increased in price by £17.50 Do you wish to accept this increase or re-order a cheaper model?
(b) Printout copier PX200 is now compatible with European and Japanese models of word processors.
(c) Stencil correction fluid is temporarily out of stock. Delivery to Micro Services is expected before the weekend. Do you wish available goods to be sent or order to be delayed until stencil correction fluid is available?

MESSAGE TAKEN BY: Sue Johnson

Note

1 The handwriting on the message form is legible. It is not customary to type phone messages so it is important that handwriting is clear.
2 A simple heading has been given at the commencement of the message. This allows the reader to identify quickly the subject of the message.
3 The message is presented in three lettered parts since the caller indicated there were three points she wished to bring to Mr Parker's attention.
4 The signature of the person who took the message is written legibly so that Mr Parker can check on any details that the message may not have made clear.

Exercises

The following are situations designed to allow three people at a time to role-play some phone calls. One should act as *caller*, another *receiver* and the third as *observer*. The observer should make notes as the call is made of good and bad points in the exchange. A discussion can then take place, after the call has been completed, concerning how improvements might be made. You do not actually need to use real phone equipment but, if old telephones are available, this would help.

Situation 1

Caller: You are confined to the house because of sickness. The doctor has visited you and left a prescription. Phone a friend to ask if he or she can call and pick up the prescription and have it prepared at a local pharmacy.
Receiver: Make sure you make polite enquiries concerning the caller's health and check when it would be convenient to call for the prescription and then return with the medicine.

Situation 2

Caller: You have heard of an interesting course at a college which a friend attends. Phone your friend and get the details of the course and the college. Find out what you can about the standards of courses at the college concerned.
Receiver: Think about the courses with which you are familiar so that you can sustain a reasonable conversation.

Situation 3

Caller: You are going for a day out on a coach with a club or group of friends. You have lost a list of the times of departure and return as well as details of places to be visited. Phone someone who has organized the day out to check on the relevant details.
Receiver: prepare a list of times and places before you take part n the call.

Situation 4

Caller: You have decided to go to the cinema. You are not sure what films are showing at your local 'unit' cinema. Phone the cinema to check what is showing, what are the times of afternoon performances and what the seat prices are. Conclude by making a booking.

Receiver: Equip yourself with an advertisement for a local 'unit' cinema or devise some titles, times and prices beforehand. Make sure that you tell the caller what is the last time that tickets can be collected.

Situation 5

Caller: Your car has broken down. You remember that a friend once told you of the name, address and phone number of a good garage in town. You need to phone the friend to check the details as you have forgotten the desired name and address.

Receiver: You should ask the caller to wait while you go and check in your address book. You may use the details of a garage in you local Yellow Pages directory or a garage that you actually know.

Comment

The three people involved in the exercises should take it in turn to be callers, receivers and observers. The caller should have a prepared message pad ready or at least some paper to note down the answer to the query made.

The receiver should prepare material beforehand so that realistic conversation may take place.

The observer should comment on whether the call was completed successfully, whether the tone of voice was appropriate, etc.

You should, after a time, be able to devise your own situations as a group and make more 'mock' phone calls.

36 Ongoing case studies

Honeypot Biscuits

Just before she was due to go home at the end of the afternoon, Sandra received the following phone call on an outside line.

Sandra: Good afternoon, Honeypot Biscuits, Sandra Kong speaking. Can I help you?

Mrs Jarvis: Hello, Sandra. This is Angela Jarvis. I'm glad I caught you. I thought I might have miscalculated the time difference.

Sandra: I still have five minutes before it's time to go hone, Angela. Is the trip going well?

Mrs Jarvis: It's going very well indeed, thank you Sandra. I've got a rather important message that I'd like you to get to Mr Simpson before he goes home please.

Sandra: Mr Simpson is on the evening shift today, Angela, so there should be no trouble getting the message to him.

Mrs Jarvis: That's excellent. As you will know from my itinerary, I'm due back in Toronto tomorrow. I'd like Mr Simpson to telex the following information to the Toronto Chamber of Commerce so that I can have it for my final meeting with Steven Cellik.

Sandra: I'm ready, Angela.

Mrs Jarvis: Fine. I need the following information. Firstly, I need to know the precise grade of oatmeal that we use in the majority of our production.

Sandra: Yes?

Mrs Jarvis: Secondly, I need to have a list of any preservatives we use in the recipes. I've just thought, Sandra –

Sandra: Yes?

Mrs Jarvis: You might get Mr Simpson to check whether the preservatives we do use are organic or chemical.

Sandra: I'll do that, Angela.

Mrs Jarvis: Next, I need figures to show our production levels over the last three years.

Sandra: Yes?

Mrs Jarvis: He'll find those in the last annual report, although he's probably got them on file anyway.

Sandra: Yes, Angela.

Mrs Jarvis: If you could ask Mr Simpson to telex that information as soon as possible, I can pick up the information when I get to Toronto tomorrow.

Sandra: I'll see that he gets the message.

Mrs Jarvis: Thanks very much, Sandra. I'll see you on Monday.

Sandra: Have a good flight. Goodbye, Angela.

Mrs Jarvis: Goodbye, Sandra.

Exercise
Using the telephone message form layout suggested in the previous chapter, fill in the details of Mrs Jarvis's call as Sandra would for Mr Simpson's attention.

Sandy Bay Leisure Services

Tracy: Good morning, Leisure Services Department, Tracy Donaldson speaking. Can I help?

Mr Bickerstaffe: Thank goodness it's you, Tracy. It's Arthur Bickerstaffe here. I've been ringing off and on for the last half hour. Where is everybody?

Tracy: I'm sorry Arthur but I've only just arrived. You haven't forgotten that you're one hour ahead of us in France have you?

Mr Bickerstaffe: Oh dear. I remembered to adjust my watch when I got here but forgot to adjust my brain this morning. Anyway, I've got a message for our friend the Finance Officer.

Tracy: The Finance Officer. Yes Arthur?

Mr Bickerstaffe: I've been having some very interesting talks with my opposite number over here in France. We've been discussing the possibility of a Twin Town Festival.

Tracy: Twin Town Festival. Yes?

Mr Bickerstaffe: Ask the Finance Officer if he will phone me at . . . let's see, 2.00 pm your time. I'll be in conference with Monsieur Onzan. The number is La Rochelle 306500.

Tracy: 2.00 pm, Monsieur Onzan, La Rochelle 306500, Is that O N Z A N?

Mr Bickerstaffe: That's correct. Tell him we need only a brief word concerning possible English Tourist Board sponsorship.

Tracy: Very well, Arthur. Fine. I'll make sure he gets the message.

Mr Bickerstaffe: And Tracy?

Tracy: Yes?

Mr Bickerstaffe: There's no need to mention that I forgot the time difference.

Tracy: Of course not.

Mr Bickerstaffe: Thanks a lot. Goodbye Tracy.

Tracy: Au revoir, Arthur.

Exercise
In either telephone message pad form or memo form, draft the message that Mr Bickerstaffe wants Tracy to pass on to the Finance Officer.

37 Electronics in the world of work

Various chapters throughout this book will have suggested the increasing importance and significance of electronics in modern business. People will always be of prime importance but the aid to speed and efficiency provided for staff by electronic processing equipment is a feature of today's world of work.

In college, school or work you will find yourself increasingly in contact (hopefully in a 'hands on' situation) with some or all of the following.

Word processors

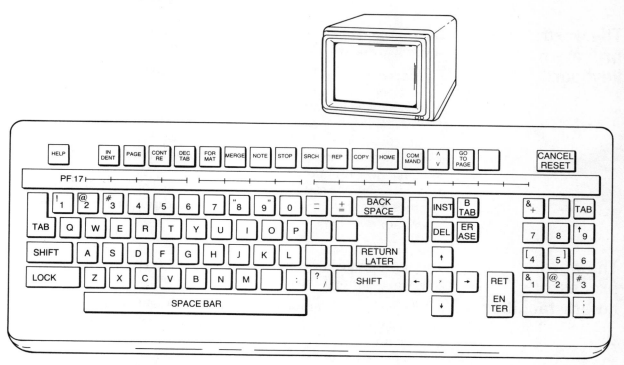

Figure 37.1   Word processor

The typing of letters, documents and other manuscripts is made easier on a word processor (Figure 37.1) for the following reasons:

1   Pressing the keys causes the characters to appear on a visual display unit screen (VDU). These characters can be adjusted if a mistake is made by simply 'overtyping' to correct the error.
2   Editing of the text is easy as deletions and insertions of words, sentences or paragraphs can be made by selecting the appropriate function on the keyboard. Margins may also be widened or narrowed with the text rearranged automatically.

3 Anything typed up on the keyboard can be stored for recall at a later date.

4 Standard or form letters, together with names and addresses, can be stored and the names and addresses inserted by the word processor with the result that an apparently personalized letter is available for every required recipient. (This feature is often given the general term 'mail merge'.)

5 The document that you have typed is only put on to paper when it is a perfect copy (according to the VDU screen). The document can then be printed out or stored until required. Greater accuracy and savings on paper costs are the logical result of this basic feature.

6 The stored text may be transmitted directly and electronically to another machine. The receiving machine may be within the business itself or somewhere else in the world. (If the word processor has this facility it is usually termed 'electronic mail'.)

The word processor keyboard

The keyboard of a word processor is split into three sections, each of which deals with a different set of functions.

1 *The standard QWERTY typewriter key section* All modern key sections will feature a backspace–correct key which allows mistakes to be edited out.

2 *The function key section* These keys tell the machine to change functions. This section will include a control–command key to let the machine know that the operator is ready to move to some new function.

3 *The cursor control keys* These allow a cursor to move along the lines of text shown on the screen and editing changes to be made.

The word processor's editing facilities

The appropriate keys on a word processor keyboard will allow the following editing functions to be carried out:

1 To move a paragraph or other block of text from one part of the page to another (or even to another part of the overall document).

2 To move the pages on display from one to another.

3 To change the lettering on display from upper case to lower case or to alter the type face.

4 To search the pages of a document for a specific word or short phrase for alteration or correction.

Mail merge

The above term has developed to describe a facility of great importance for the modern office. Different terms exist with which you may be more familiar: *form letters*, standard letters, variable reader codes, batched infill. Whatever name is used, the result is the same in effect.

1 The operator designs a *standard, frequently used* letter with all the required information. Where there are individual variable details (name, address, time, salutation, etc) a *variable* or *merge*

mark is made. This standard letter with 'electronic spaces' is stored for later additions (see Figure 37.2).

2 The operator makes a *list of the variables* that are to be merged into the standard letter. These variables must each be separated by a variable or merge mark. It is obvious that for every variable or merge mark in the original letter there must be a variable in the list (see Figure 37.3).

```
&name
&address1
&address2
&address3
&postcode


Dear &name

Thank  you  for  your  letter  of  &date  ,  and  we
are  sorry  to  hear  of  your  dissatisfaction
with  our  &product1.

If  you  would  like  to  call  in  at  our  &location
office  and  ask  for  &contact  ,  I  am  sure  we
will  be  able  to  resolve  your  problem.

Yours  sincerely



Tarrif  Kalei
Customer  Relation
```

Figure 37.2   The standard letter with merge marks   You should note that different word processors and mail merge operations utilise slightly different symbols and methods; the principle is in all cases the same.

```
1    Mr A Brown, 9 Park Road, Mitcham,  Surrey,
MS9 4CB,   6 July, personal computer, Mitcham,
Mr Singh
2   Ms  C  Clarkson,    115   Morley   Crescent,
Crowthorpe, Essex, CE11 5WB, 2 July, computer
disk drive, Barking, Mrs Rogers
3
 "
 "
 "
 "
 "
 "
```

Figure 37.3   The file of variables   The actual names or words are listed in the same order as the variable names in the main letter; note that different mail merge systems operate in slightly different ways, but the principle is in all cases the same.

The standard letter is merged at the printout stage with the variables which results in a series of apparently individually written letters.

Electronic file handling

Developments in electronics and magnetic storage tape have led to information being easily stored and retrieved via information processing systems.

The different forms of information that could be filed in the electronic system will include:

1 Reports, correspondence, documents.
2 Specifications and other data.
3 Telex and electronic mail correspondence.
4 Programmes for other aspects of the system.

Database management

Different files of information stored electronically obviously require some aspects of the information to be repeated on the record for retrieval. Some information will need to be held by different departments within an organization and when an individual department alters some of the facts on store it is important that only that department's record is altered (eg details of personnel, addresses, sales, stocks, etc).

An information storage and retrieval system based on hard or floppy disk storage software and which controls a variety of programmes is called a Database Management System. If an individual or department requires information, the employee responsible for operating the computer is approached with the particular request. With a suitable program key, the information is quickly retrieved.

Aspects of electronic file handling

1 Most file systems are operated by two disk drives.
   (a) A system drive that allows the particular programs to be put into operation.
   (b) A work drive that holds the information on data files.
2 Database management systems allow programs to give access only to the particular data that is required instead of surveying the whole field of information held on record.
3 Limitations on a system's memory capacity have been overcome by the use of 'virtual operating systems' which divide all the files held and the programs into equal size, small pages.
4 The effect of 'virtual operating systems' is to allow apparently unlimited RAM for an individual user of the files.

Electronic mail

Most automated offices now have electronic mail facility as a standard feature. This provides the following advantages:

1 Letters, memos and other documents created on a word processor can be sent electronically to an address inside the

system (another part of the organization) or to another machine in some distant part of the country or overseas.

2   Letters, memos and other documents received by the electronic mail system can be read from the VDU or printed out.

3   Speed and accuracy are inevitable aspects of the electronic mail (assuming accuracy on the part of the sender).

4   Easy access is another attraction of the electronic mail system. A portable microcomputer linked into a telephone system allows access to the electronic mail at any time and wherever you may be.

FAX

Facsimile transmission (FAX) is an electronic means by which an image or document is transmitted with speed and accuracy.

The image or document to be transmitted is scanned electronically and converted into a signal. The signal is then transmitted and converted back into the original by the equipment at the destination (which may be thousands of miles away if necessary).

For most of this century machines have existed that can perform the above functions but only recently has the technology been developed to a state of such speed and accuracy of reproduction.

By analogue or digital transmission, machines can now transmit an A4 sized document or image in under two minutes. The accuracy is such that signatures transmitted by FAX are legally acceptable.

The linking of FAX machines to word processors is a significant new development which will allow the filing of image or verbal documents as well as having implications for document delivery.

Index